R. W. Franklin received his Ph.D. from
Northwestern University, was Assistant Professor of English at the University of Wisconsin, and is currently teaching abroad.

The Editing of Emily Dickinson

R. W. FRANKLIN

The Editing of Emily Dickinson

A RECONSIDERATION

MADISON, MILWAUKEE, AND LONDON

THE UNIVERSITY OF WISCONSIN PRESS 1967

Published by the University of
Wisconsin Press
Madison, Milwaukee, and London
U.S.A.: Box 1379, Madison, Wisconsin 53701
U.K.: 26–28 Hallam Street, London, W. 1
Copyright © 1967 by the Regents of
the University of Wisconsin
Printed in the United States of America by
American Book–Stratford Press, Inc.
Library of Congress Catalog Card Number 67–13558

To EGG, LG, and RVC

Acknowledgments

I have been helped often during the preparation of this book. I am particularly indebted to the Amherst College Library, to Newton F. McKeon, the Director, and to Floyd Merritt of the staff. I have the permission of the Amherst College Library to quote from its Emily Dickinson collection and to reproduce the illustrations in Figures 1–5, 7–20, 22–24, and 26–27. I wish to thank the Houghton Library of Harvard University for generous assistance and for permission to use the illustrations in Figures 6, 21, and 28. The illustration in Figure 25 is included through the courtesy of the Wellesley College Library, which also granted permission to quote from a letter in its collections. For patience and expertise I owe much to the University of Massachusetts Photograph Center and the Wisconsin State Crime Laboratory.

My thanks are due to Millicent Todd Bingham for encouragement and for permission to quote from the unpublished letters, diaries, and journals of her mother, Mabel Loomis Todd. Part of my research was supported by grants from the Danforth Foundation, Northwestern University, and the University of Wisconsin. To the many others who helped, I would like to express my appreciation, especially to those who read the work in manuscript and offered suggestions: Richard V. Carter, Wallace W. Douglas, LaVerne Goman, Harrison Hayford, Ernest Samuels, G. Thomas Tanselle, and Martha J. Vicinus. I should perhaps note here that a good deal of the research for this book was completed by 1965 and was copyrighted in the author's name in that year.

I gratefully acknowledge permission of the publishers, Harper & Row, to quote from Millicent Todd Bingham, *Ancestors' Brocades: The Literary Debut of Emily Dickinson* (1945) and from *Letters of Emily Dickinson* (1931), edited by Mabel Loomis Todd. Eight complete poems (nos. 19, 297, 331, 621, 681, 947, 992, and 1712) and parts of others are reprinted by permission of the publishers and the Trustees of Amherst College from Thomas H. Johnson, Editor, *The Poems of Emily Dickinson,* Cambridge, Mass.: The Belknap Press of Harvard University Press, Copyright, 1951, 1955, by The President and Fellows of Harvard College. *Merkur* has kindly granted permission to quote Emily Dickinson's poem "It's like the light" as it appears in Kurt Oppens, "Emily Dickinson: Überlieferung und Prophetie," *Merkur,* XIV (January 1960), 17–40.

R. W. F.

March 1967

Contents

Illustrations

Tables and Chart

Introduction

Emily Dickinson did not publish. Except for a handful of poems, apparently made public against her wishes, her work remained unpublished during her lifetime. Whatever her reasons for silence may have been, she nevertheless pursued poetry devotedly, and at her death in 1886 she left a large group of manuscript poems in various states of completion. Her sister, Lavinia, destroyed the correspondence that she found, as was the custom, but the poems she decided were Emily's letter to the world. These, to our permanent literary debt, she did not burn.

Unsatisfied while the poems were unpublished, Lavinia set herself to finding an editor. She found two: Mabel Loomis Todd, wife of an Amherst College astronomy professor, and Thomas Wentworth Higginson, well-known writer and critic who had known the poet during her lifetime. With some hesitation, they agreed to edit a volume. Mrs. Todd copied the poems from the manuscripts and made a preliminary selection. Both she and Colonel Higginson changed the unorthodox punctuation and altered readings in an effort to gain public acceptance for the poems. Their collaboration produced *Poems by Emily Dickinson* (1890), a slim volume of 116 poems that aroused the literary world. Sales were extraordinary, and the editors issued a second series the following year. Without Colonel Higginson's assistance, Mrs. Todd edited a collection of Emily Dickinson's letters (1894) and a third series of the poems (1896). These marked the end of the nineteenth-century volumes.

The editorial history that followed was confusing. When Mrs. Todd and Colonel Higginson edited the poems, the manuscripts that had been in Emily Dickinson's possession at her death were yet intact. Near the end of the century, however, Mrs. Todd and Lavinia Dickinson had a legal and emotional quarrel about a strip of land in Amherst claimed by both. As a result, shortly after the third series was published in 1896, Mrs. Todd ceased working on the poems, and the manuscripts themselves were split between her and Lavinia.

This division of the manuscripts in the nineteenth century led to editorial confusion in the twentieth. For many years Mrs. Todd's share of the manuscripts was packed away out of the reach of publication. Lavinia's share, however, passed to Susan Dickinson, the poet's sister-in-law, and then to Martha Dickinson Bianchi, her niece, who issued a bewildering series of editions, each supposedly exhausting the unpublished manuscripts. *The Single Hound,* containing poems Emily Dickinson had sent to Susan, appeared in 1914 and, together with the three nineteenth-century editions, formed *The Complete Poems of Emily Dickinson* (1924). *Further Poems,* however, came out in 1929 and was soon collected into another "complete" edition, *The Poems of Emily Dickinson* (1930). Still more poems appeared in 1935 in *Unpublished Poems,* and another collected edition followed two years later. When Mrs. Bianchi died in 1943, the manuscript poems in her possession had, for the most part, been published. But many of those in Mrs. Todd's share of the manuscripts had not been, and in 1945 Millicent Todd Bingham, daughter of the first editor, released to a surprised public *Bolts of Melody*—over 650 hitherto unpublished poems. At the same time Mrs. Bingham published a companion volume,

Ancestors' Brocades, in which she told the story of the early editing, the lawsuit, and the confusion that followed.

In 1950 Harvard University acquired Lavinia's part of the manuscripts and also claimed ownership, by right of the purchase agreement with Mrs. Bianchi's heir, of the manuscripts in Mrs. Bingham's possession. Though her ownership was contested, Mrs. Bingham allowed Thomas H. Johnson to use them, and for the first time since the 1890's both portions of the manuscripts were available to the same editor. Mr. Johnson subsequently published the three-volume variorum, *The Poems of Emily Dickinson* (1955), the most significant of all the editions. Mr. Johnson's purpose was to publish all the poems— edited from the manuscripts, not reprinted from other sources— and to present them literally, as written, without alteration however well-intentioned. Mr. Johnson, moreover, sought to recount the publishing history of each poem and to provide all the variant readings, critically compared with the extant manuscripts.

The effect of the variorum upon Dickinson scholarship has been prodigious. No longer hampered by a bewildering array of editions, texts, and variants, Dickinson scholarship has flourished in the past dozen years. Quite rightly, Mr. Johnson's edition has been highly acclaimed; it is an important achievement. Yet there is still work to be done. Mrs. Todd's transcripts, her typewriters, her diaries and journals, as well as the manuscripts themselves have fresh contributions to make to our understanding of Emily Dickinson's poetry and how we should edit it. Mr. Johnson has established the center; the aim of this study is to add to the circumference.

The Editing of Emily Dickinson

CHAPTER I

1886–1891: Editorial Procedure for the First and Second Series

The nineteenth-century editing of Emily Dickinson's poetry may be divided into two phases of equal length: 1886–91 and 1891–96. The two phases did not divide sharply, but overlapped in midsummer 1891. At that time Mabel Loomis Todd, Emily Dickinson's friend and first editor, was working steadily on the poems. The copy for *Poems, Second Series* (1891), the last volume she was to edit with Thomas Wentworth Higginson's help, was given her final reading and dispatched to him on July 13, 1891. Before proof arrived, Mrs. Todd surveyed the poems that Emily Dickinson had bound into fascicles and began putting the Dickinson materials—manuscripts and transcripts—into manageable order. These tasks when finished would complete the first phase. Meanwhile, Mrs. Todd initiated the second phase when she turned her attention to a third series. She had earlier contemplated such a volume, having predicted in her diary the previous January that "there will yet be *ten* volumes of her poems,"[1] and, because of her manner of copying, had even accomplished some of the editing; but she took the first step toward the new series, not to appear until 1896, when she made a preliminary selection on July 16, 1891.[2]

COLONEL HIGGINSON AND
MABEL LOOMIS TODD

The first phase had begun five years earlier. Shortly after Emily Dickinson's death on May 15, 1886, her sister, Lavinia, found a locked box containing seven hundred of Emily's poems,[3] carefully copied on folded sheets of stationery and bound into fascicles of four or five sheets.[4] Convinced that her sister had rare talent, Lavinia determined that the poems should be published. Since appeals to Susan Dickinson, the sister-in-law, did not achieve that aim, she recruited for her crusade, as she liked to call it, outside the Dickinson family. She turned to Mrs. Todd and also to Thomas Wentworth Higginson, whom Emily had known, mainly through correspondence, for over twenty years. A poet, essayist, reformer, and well-known arbiter of nineteenth-century taste, Higginson had received a request from Emily in 1862 at the height of her emotional crisis to tell her whether or not her verse were alive. He responded, and she became his devoted "scholar" and he her "preceptor." Though they met but twice, the relationship lasted until Emily's death, and Colonel Higginson came to Amherst to read at her funeral "Last Lines," Emily Brontë's poem on immortality. Lavinia's petition, however, did not move Colonel Higginson to action. Already past sixty, he replied that he was too busy to wrestle with the difficulties of the manuscripts and that he doubted enough suitable poems could be found to fill a volume.[5]

Finding no encouragement from that quarter except a promise by Higginson to go over the poems if they were put in shape for consideration, Lavinia increasingly pressed Mrs. Todd to have them published, for apart from Sue, she seemed the only person in Amherst qualified for the job. In 1881 David Peck Todd, an 1875 graduate of Amherst College, had returned to his alma mater as Instructor in Astronomy and Director of the Observatory, bringing with him his young wife, whose presence in Amherst created a stir. Just twenty-four and fresh from the social rounds of Washington, Mabel Loomis Todd found the rural Massachusetts town decidedly slow and the four thousand people who lived there "more absorbed in the severities of living than in its gayeties."[6] "Everything," she wrote in her journal, "is so different from my former life—& yet it is pleasant, too."[7] Her education had included a finishing school in fashionable Georgetown, where she had learned that card playing, dancing, and intelligent conversation were part of a lady's accomplishments, and she had studied piano, voice, and harmony at the New England Conservatory of Music in Boston. Mrs. Todd shortly came to regard Amherst with affection, and in the town she gave fully of her energy and talent—speaking, entertaining, performing frequently—and offered lessons in singing and piano as well as in painting, at which she was also proficient.

Mrs. Todd's accomplishments together with her charm and vivacity soon attracted the attention of the Dickinson sisters, and for several years before Emily Dickinson's death Mrs. Todd would sing for them and play selections from Beethoven, Scarlatti, and Bach—composers apparently unfamiliar to the sisters, but greatly pleasing to them.[8] Actually Mrs. Todd never met Emily face-to-face, for the poet would not venture closer than the dark hall next to the drawing room. But the two unusual women liked each other, trading poems and paintings to show their regard. Though in 1886 Mrs. Todd had known Emily Dickinson for less than five years and had never seen her closely, at the poet's death she was "full of grief."[9]

Lavinia's appeal for help with the poems had the full force of friendship, but Mrs. Todd also hesitated when presented with seven hundred poems to edit:

> Having already had some experience with publishers, I told her that no one would attempt to read them in Emily's own peculiar handwriting, much less judge them; that I should have to copy them all, then have them passed upon like any other literary production, from the commercial standpoint of the publishing business, and that certainly not less than a year must elapse before they could possibly be brought out.[10]

Part of her hesitation came from a feeling that the poems' "unconventionality might repel publishers,"[11] but much of it was caused by her own literary aspirations. Even before Emily's death and Lavinia's importunity, Mrs. Todd had confessed in her journal "a perfect passion all the time to write,"[12] and she had already published some articles and stories. Editing Emily's poetry could interfere with her own work, for, as she knew, she had more ideas than time in which to realize them: "Trying to write a little, my brain teeming, and only a quarter enough time. . . . I ought to be four."[13] At length, however, sometime during 1887, she yielded to Lavinia's imperatives and accepted the task which understandably gave her pause. Not one, but more than three years elapsed before a volume appeared and nearly ten before Mrs. Todd ceased working on the poems Lavinia brought to her. Whether her own literary hopes suffered because of the editing is hard to determine. She published extensively during the following years—stories, reviews, travel letters, articles, and books, which ranged from "Women in Hawaii" to "Tripoli and Her People," from "Some Aspects of College Professors" to "Witchcraft in New England," "The Passion Play of 1900," and *Total Eclipses of the Sun*. But certainly her own work was not the literary equal of Emily Dickinson's. If Mrs. Todd was partially denied a literary career because of her editing of Emily Dickinson's poetry, that denial also afforded her a permanent niche in the history of American literature.

COPYING THE POEMS

Full-scale copying of the poems could not begin at once. The National Academy of Sciences had appointed David Todd chief of the United States expedition to Japan to observe the total eclipse of the sun during August 1887, and Mrs. Todd was to accompany him. They left Amherst in early June, returning on the thirteenth of October.[14] Work on the poems apparently started in earnest about November, for by the thirtieth of that month Mrs. Todd could remark in her diary for the first time since her return that she had copied "two or three *more* of Emily's poems."[15] A recent biographer of Higginson, Anna

Mary Wells, argues that the Colonel was responsible for initiating the actual work on the poems. When he visited in Amherst in July 1888, Higginson talked with Lavinia Dickinson about publishing them. Mrs. Wells speculates that Lavinia, so encouraged, demanded that Sue return the box of manuscripts and that she then took them to Mrs. Todd.[16] The above diary entry, however, shows that Mrs. Todd had already begun copying the preceding fall, and there are other entries that record her efforts between then and Higginson's coming to town in July.[17]

Frequently Mrs. Todd devoted three or four morning hours to the poems, yet the task seemed interminable to her:

> I wrote and wrote and wrote. For nearly a year I translated them into typewriter MSS. Then I had to give up the Hammond I had used, and I wrote a few on the little "World" machine, but that was rather slow.[18]

Though still an imperfect invention, the typewriter promised relief from the drudgery of the pen, and for the first year, as this journal entry explains, Mrs. Todd transcribed mechanically. Figures 1 and 2 are typescripts of poems published in the third series (1896), but copied at this time, 1887–88.[19] The first, "I live with Him—I see His face" (V463),* is one of 175 copied on the Hammond typewriter with a black ribbon, the most common form of typescript. For a brief time Mrs. Todd used a purple ribbon on this machine, and some twenty of the forty typescripts made with it are still extant.[20] Figure 2, "Poor little Heart!" (V192) transcribed on the World machine,[21] shows Mrs. Todd's second mode of copying. It apparently started late in 1888 and continued into 1889. The World, a more primitive machine than the Hammond, had only capitals and was operated by rotating a letter into place and pressing down—slow and tedious work indeed—yet the "few" Mrs. Todd did on this machine totaled nearly ninety. All forty of those extant have purple ink.

* For convenience, Emily Dickinson's poems will be cited with their variorum numbering, indicated by a *V*.

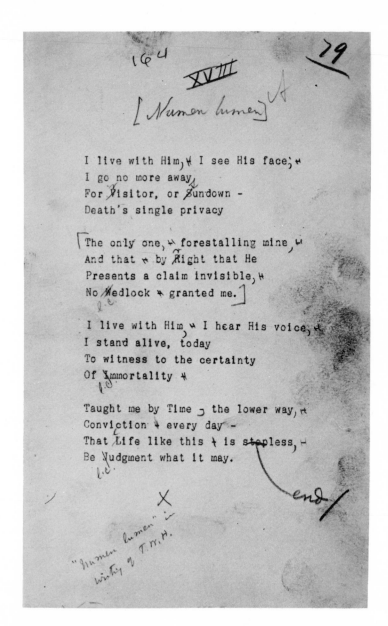

Fig. 1.—Hammond typescript of "I live with Him—I see His face" (V463). By permission of the Amherst College Library.

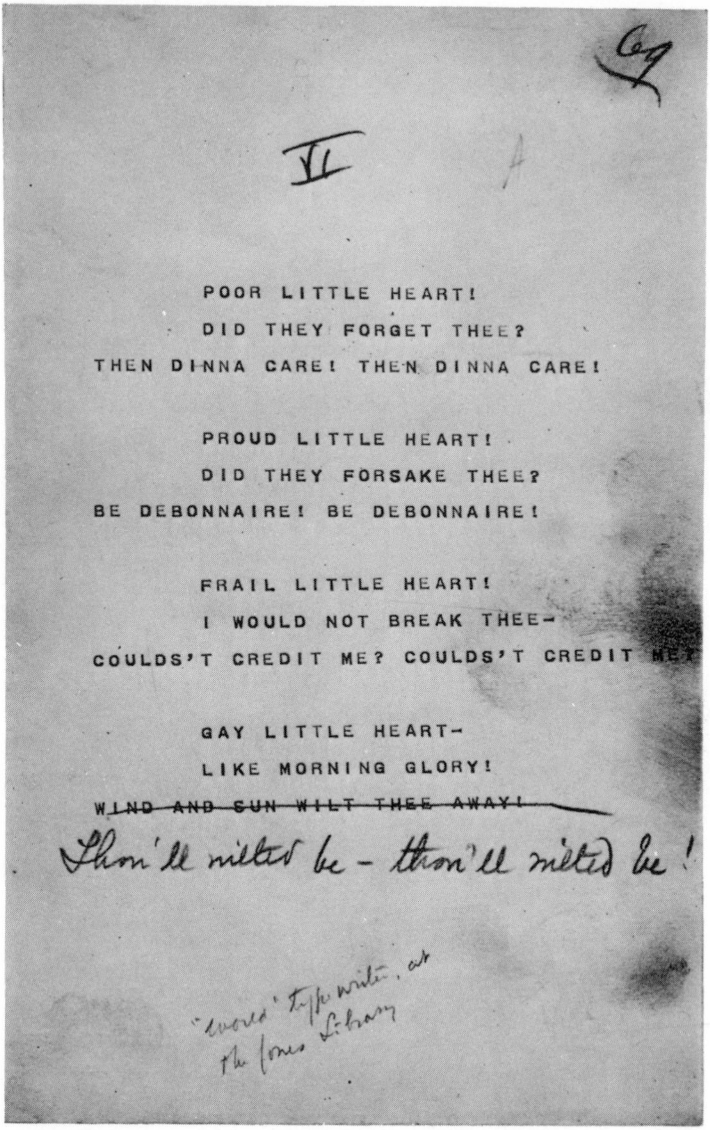

Fig. 2.—World typescript of "Poor little Heart!" (V192). By permission of the Amherst College Library.

My figures for the number of transcripts made by these two typewriters are approximate as well as conjectural, for many transcripts are no longer available, having served in the printer's copies for *Poems* (1890) and (1891) and then having been destroyed. Even though many are now lost, when the surviving transcripts are placed in correspondence with the packets from which they were copied, a pattern usually emerges that indicates the medium as well as the paper used for those missing.

PACKET 40

Sheet	Poem	Surviving Transcripts
H 214a	V455	. . . .
b	V617	Hammond (black) on paper X
c	V456	Hammond (black) on paper X
d	V618	Hammond (black) on paper X
H 215a	V457	Hammond (black) on paper X
b	V619	. . . .
c	V620	. . . .
d	V621	. . . .
H 216a	V622	. . . .
b	V623	. . . .
c	V624	Hammond (black) on paper X
H 217a	V625	. . . .
b	V626	Hammond (black) on paper X
c	V458	Hammond (black) on paper X
d	V459	Hammond (black) on paper X
H 218a	V460	Hammond (black) on paper X
b	V627	Hammond (black) on paper X
H 219a	V461	Hammond (black) on paper X
b	V462	Hammond (black) on paper X
c	V463	Hammond (black) on paper X
d	V464	Hammond (black) on paper X

Table 1.—Transcript pattern for packet 40. The packet has twenty-one poems on six sheets. Fourteen of the transcripts survive, forming the above pattern. The other seven transcripts were used as copy for *poems* (1890) or (1891) and presumably have been destroyed. (The sheet numbers are those assigned by the Houghton Library; the lower case letters simply indicate the order of poems on a given sheet.)

For example, seven poems in packet 40 (Table 1) were published in the first or second series and now have no transcripts,
yet, like the surviving transcripts for packet 40, they were most
likely copied with the Hammond (black ribbon) onto the paper
that I have here called X. Similarly, all of the poems in packet
2 that lack transcripts (Table 2) were published in 1890 or

PACKET 2

Sheet	Poem	Surviving Transcripts
H 5a	V59	World (purple) on paper Y
b	V148	World (purple) on paper Y
c	V100	World (purple) on paper Y
d	V101	. . . . . .
e	V102	World (purple) on paper Y
H 6a	V103	Hammond (black) on paper Y
b	V104	Hammond (black) on paper Y
c	V149	. . . .
d	V105	Hammond (black) on paper Y
e	V106	. . . .
H 7a	V60	Hammond (black) on paper Y
b	V61	Hammond (black) on paper Y
c	V107	. . . .
d	V62	Hammond (black) on paper Y
e	V150	. . . .
f	V63	Hammond (black) on paper Y
g	V108	. . . .
H 8a	V64	. . . .
b	V109	Hammond (black) on paper Y
c	V65	Hammond (black) on paper Y

Table 2.—Transcript pattern for packet 2. The seven poems with missing
transcripts were published in 1890 or 1891.

1891. Since all of the surviving transcripts for sheet H 5* were
done on the World typewriter on paper Y, the missing transcript

* Here, as elsewhere in this book, I use the sheet numbers assigned
by the Houghton Library. Lower case letters (as in H 5d) merely refer
to the order of poems on a sheet. Thus H 5d indicates the fourth poem
on the sheet numbered 5 at the Houghton Library.

for this sheet (H 5d: V101) was probably also done on the World typewriter on paper Y. Mrs. Todd used the same paper when copying the remaining sheets in the packet, but the transcripts were undoubtedly made not on the World machine but on the Hammond.

Thomas H. Johnson, the variorum editor of Emily Dickinson's poetry, explains that "Mrs. Todd began copying systematically, starting with the poems in the packet that her husband had numbered one."[22] This explanation needs two corrections. First, the variorum editor has probably erred in identifying the handwriting on the packets: they were, in all likelihood, numbered not by David Todd but by his wife.[23] Second, Mr. Johnson's account of the copying procedure must be wrong. Mrs. Todd could not have started with the packet numbered one and proceeded systematically, for packet 1 (Table 3) was transcribed on the World machine, Mrs. Todd's second mode of copying, in 1888 or 1889, at least a year after the work had begun.

Mrs. Todd worked first on the Hammond typewriter and used it, with black or purple ribbon, for all or parts of fifteen packets.[24] If she had started the copying with packet 1 and proceeded systematically, the packets copied on the Hammond would have been those numbered 1 to 15. But they are not. The Hammond machine was used on packets 2, 4–7, 9, 13–15, 17, 23, 26, 30, 40, and 85. Approximately 215 poems were so copied. Mrs. Todd turned to the World typewriter when she had to give up the Hammond, and the ninety transcripts done on the World, which brought the total typed to over three hundred, came from seven packets whose numbers mesh or overlap with those she had already copied: 1–3, 15, 80, 83, and 85. The order and range of these typescripts show that Mrs. Todd did not in fact copy systematically starting with packet 1. They argue, furthermore, that the numbering itself was done, not when the poems were first received, but after all had been copied.

Further support for these two assertions comes from a survey of the work done by Mrs. Todd's assistant. More than a year had elapsed since Mrs. Todd began copying the poems, more

PACKET 1

Sheet	Poem	Surviving Transcripts
H 1a	V58	. . . . . .
b	V89	. . . . . .
c	V90	. . . . . .
d	V91	. . . . . .
e	V92	World (purple) on paper Z
f	V93	. . . . . .
H 2a	V94	. . . . . .
b	V95	. . . . . .
c	V96	World (purple) on paper Z
d	V97	World (purple) on paper Z
e	V98	. . . . . .
f	V88	. . . . . .
g	V99	. . . . . .
h	V903	. . . . . .
H 3a	V11	World (purple) on paper Z
b	V49	. . . . . .
c	V50	World (purple) on paper Z
d	V51	World (purple) on paper Z
H 4a	V12	. . . . . .
b	V52	. . . . . .
c	V53	. . . . . .
d	V13	. . . . . .
e	V54	. . . . . .
f	V55	World (purple) on paper Z

Table 3.—Transcript pattern for packet 1. There is a partial transcript for H 1c and for H 4a, apparently false starts, also done on the World (purple) on paper Z.

than three hundred poems had been typed, but the volume was not out, and "Vinnie began to get impatient."[25] Mrs. Todd, trying to hasten things for her, hired an assistant:

> I got one, & she did perhaps a hundred poems—but I could not stand it. The absolute lack of any approach to understanding or sympathy in what she was copying, although she did mechanically well enough, made poor Miss Graves seem to me a shade worse than an insentiate [insentient] machine—and some of her mistakes in Emily's

> mad words were so ludicrous as to be pathetic. Besides it took more time to put her copies into fit shape than to do it all myself.[26]

Harriet Graves[27] served as a copyist, by hand, for about five months in 1889. Mrs. Todd in her diary mentioned her first on the seventh of March when "Miss Graves called about poems," on the ninth, and again on the tenth when she "got last of poems from Miss Graves." On July 14, Mrs. Todd "finished up a volume of the poems—correcting after the girl," and on July 22, 1889, she made a final, simple entry about her: "Miss Graves on business."[28]

Figure 3, part of a transcript of "I cried at Pity—not at Pain" (V588), is an example of Harriet Graves' work.[29] Apparently lacking appreciation of Emily Dickinson's poetry, Miss Graves nevertheless "did mechanically well enough." She in fact copied more than Mrs. Todd's estimate of one hundred poems; some 141 of her transcripts are yet extant, and the distribution of these transcripts when they are set in correspondence with the packets indicates that the original number was close to 180. She did all or part of eleven packets: 5, 8, 17–19, 21–22, 27, 29, 31, and 34.

The packet range of her transcripts confirms the view that the packets were not copied in the order of their numbering and that the numbering itself was done after the copying. Miss Graves was hired about March 1889, nearly a year and a half after the copying got under way. By then Mrs. Todd was clearly farther along than packet 5 or packet 8, the first of the numbered packets from which Miss Graves made transcripts. As has been shown, Mrs. Todd had already typed over three hundred poems. That packets 1–7 contain fewer than half that number indicates that the order of numbering and the order of copying do not correspond.

Sometime in 1889 Mrs. Todd, who found Harriet Graves worse than a machine, also turned to the drudgery of the pen and found, surprisingly, that "that was quicker."[30] Harriet Graves was dismissed, perhaps in July, and later in the summer of 1889 Mrs. Todd herself copied by hand "the last one of the seven hundred."[31]

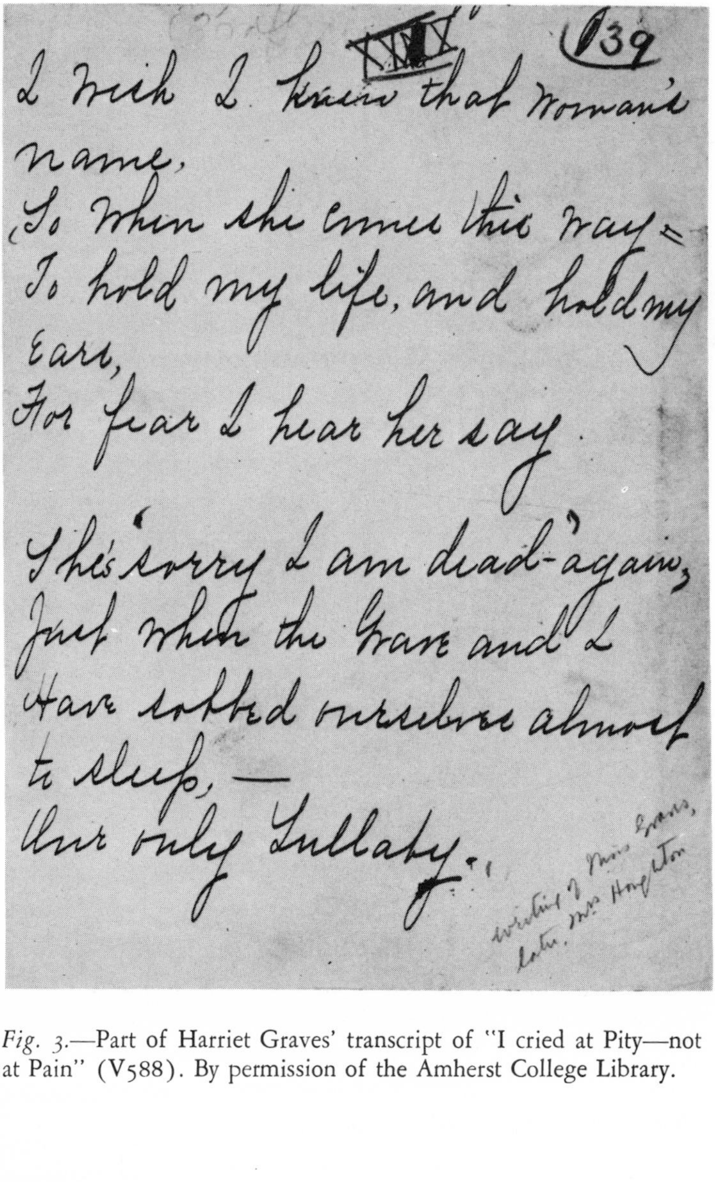

139

I wish I knew that woman's
name,
So when she comes this way—
To hold my life, and hold my
Ears,
For fear I hear her say

She's "sorry I am dead"—again,
Just when the Grave and I
Have sobbed ourselves almost
to sleep,—
Our only Lullaby.

writing of Miss Graves, later Mrs Houghton

Fig. 3.—Part of Harriet Graves' transcript of "I cried at Pity—not at Pain" (V588). By permission of the Amherst College Library.

CHARACTERISTICS OF THE TRANSCRIPTS

Most of the handwriting on the two typescripts reproduced in Figures 1 and 2 is editorial marking put there when the poems were prepared for press in 1895. Mrs. Todd revered accuracy, and she tried to be faithful at the time of copying, only introducing changes later, as in line 15 of "I live with Him—I see His face" (Fig. 1), where, sometime in 1895, she altered "stopless" to "endless." With the Hammond typewriter, one of the earliest to have small letters as well as capitals, she could even adhere somewhat faithfully to Emily Dickinson's capricious use of capitals, and in this transcript she copied many that later had to be eliminated. Having only capitals, the World machine, however, was not capable of a literal rendering. "Poor little Heart!" (Fig. 2) is but one of many that went to the printer for him to decide when to use upper or lower case.

When she took up the pen, Mrs. Todd could of course closely approach a literal copy, but she did not. Figures 4 and 5—"I had a daily Bliss" (V1057) from packet 90[32] and Mrs. Todd's transcript of it[33]—illustrate the nature of her routine copying. Emily Dickinson had left a good many poems unfinished in that she had not decided among her own alternate readings. Mrs. Todd at times passed upon these alternates when she copied the poems; at other times she deferred judgment by transcribing them, as in line 7 of this transcript where she entered both readings—"Enlarged" and "Increased"—one atop the other. She omitted the capitals on "Bliss" and "Hight" and corrected the spelling of the latter. As for punctuation, she retained Emily Dickinson's dash in line 3, but added a comma to line 2, another in line 5, and put a period at the end of the poem instead of what is probably a dash.[34]

A routine copy, then, was an attempt at an accurate text, with some of the poet's alternate readings transcribed and some eliminated, with spelling corrected, many capitals omitted, and most of the punctuation of the manuscript regularized or otherwise changed. If typed on the Hammond, however, it was generally closer to the manuscript form than if rendered in full caps on the World or if handwritten.

The transcript of "I had a daily Bliss" was copied in ink. Later with pencil Mrs. Todd prepared the poem for press. She assigned "Lost Joy" for a title and, deciding between the alternate readings in line 7, crossed out "Increased." A dash was added at the end of line 7 and commas at the end of lines 4 and 5. To effect a second *abcb* rhyme instead of an *aabc,* Mrs. Todd replaced "height" with "crag" and altered the final line as shown in Figure 5. It should be emphasized that all of these changes were later editing, done in pencil, and that the transcript itself was a faithful copy of Emily Dickinson's text with only the routine changes introduced. An editor can rely on the textual accuracy of transcripts—allowing for unintentional misreadings of course—if he ignores penciled emendations or other changes clearly made later than the time of the original copying.[35]

The 90, in lead pencil, at the foot of this transcript was placed there by Mrs. Todd to indicate in which of Emily Dickinson's packets the poem was located; many, but not all, of the transcripts have such guides. The numbers, written in blue pencil, in the upper right of Figures 1, 2, 3, and 5 were part of the pagination of the 1896 printer's copy, while the Roman numerals indicate the order of poems within the four topical sections of that volume. *Numen Lumen,* the title shown in Figure 1, was supplied by Colonel Higginson, and the *A* on the same transcript indicates that the poem was given top ranking by the editors. The number *164* at the top and the *X* at the bottom of this sheet were put there by Arlo Bates and will be discussed shortly. The explanatory notes at the foot of the transcripts in Figures 1, 2, and 3 are in the writing of Millicent Todd Bingham, the daughter of Mrs. Todd, and were added in the present century.

ROBERTS BROTHERS AND ARLO BATES

Not long after the copying of poems was finished, David Todd sailed on another eclipse expedition, this time to West Africa. Mrs. Todd did not accompany him, since women were not allowed on a combat vessel, but spent the winter of 1889–90

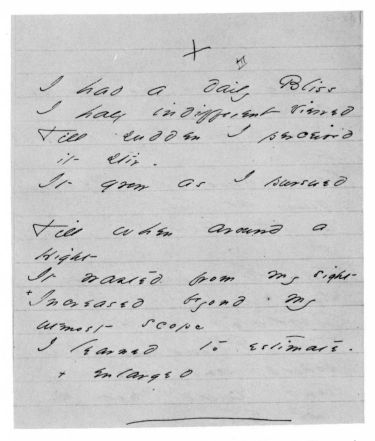

Fig. 4.—Holograph of "I had a daily Bliss" (V1057). By permission of the Amherst College Library.

in Boston, where she and Colonel Higginson conferred about editing and publishing the poems. Mrs. Todd agreed to divide the selections she had taken to him into three classes according to merit—A, B, C—and gave them, so classified, to him in November. Higginson, though enthusiastic about the project, was not well during that winter. Reading, selecting, and topically classifying the poems occupied him until spring. It was not until April 8, 1890, that he could write to Lavinia that, for the moment, he was finished with the poems and was ready for

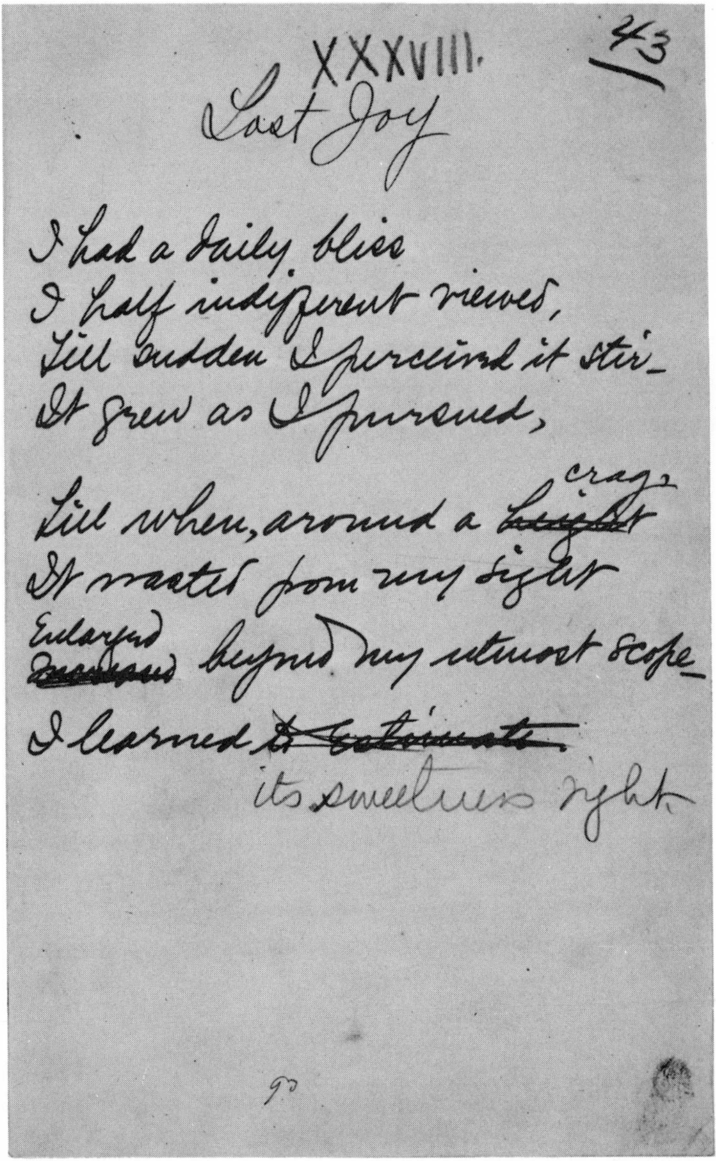

XXXVIII.

Last Joy

I had a daily bliss
I half indifferent viewed,
Till sudden I perceived it stir—
It grew as I pursued,

                                    crag
Till when, around a ~~height~~
It wasted from my sight
Enlarged
~~Bankrupt~~ beyond my utmost scope—
I learned ~~its estimate~~
                        its sweetness right

Fig. 5.—Mabel Loomis Todd's transcript of "I had a daily Bliss"
(V1057). By permission of the Amherst College Library.

Mrs. Todd to consider what he had done:

> I have selected & arranged about 200 poems, classified
> as follows

Life	44
Love	23
Nature	60
Time & Eternity	72
	199

> Now I should be glad to have Mrs. Todd go over
> them again. What is her present address? She was going
> to Chicago.[36]

In mid-March Mrs. Todd had gone to Chicago to visit a cousin.
She did not return to Amherst until mid-May, when her husband
returned from Africa. Again she and Higginson discussed the
poems, adding a few, and late in the same month they were
submitted to Thomas Niles, the head of Roberts Brothers and
a person who had encouraged Emily Dickinson to publish.[37]
The response was only a little more encouraging than the rejection already received from Houghton Mifflin.

On the advice of the poet Arlo Bates, who not only published
with Roberts Brothers but was also their reader, the firm agreed
to a small edition if Lavinia would pay for the plates. "It has
always seemed to me," Niles wrote to Higginson, "that it would
be unwise to perpetuate Miss Dickinson's poems. They are quite
as remarkable for defects as for beauties & are generally devoid
of true poetical qualities."[38] Lavinia reportedly was indignant
at this denial of her sister's talent, but she agreed to the offer.
Niles' criticism, in the light of his earlier attempts to persuade
Emily Dickinson to publish, seems excessively stern. His severity,
to some extent, was probably assumed in order to secure commercial advantage for his firm, for even the criticism he had
received from Arlo Bates, though nearsighted and limited by
the literary taste of the era, was generous as well as severe. Bates'
memorandum to Niles struck the tone of blended praise and
censure characteristic of most nineteenth-century estimates of
Emily Dickinson's poetry:

There is hardly one of these poems which does not bear marks of unusual and remarkable talent; there is hardly one of them which is not marked by an extraordinary crudity of workmanship. The author was a person of power which came very near to that indefinable quality which we call genius. She never learned her art, and constantly one is impelled to wonder and to pity at the same time. Had she published, and been forced by ambition and perhaps by need into learning the technical part of her art, she would have stood at the head of American singers. As it is she has put upon paper what reminded her of a mood or an emotion, and in nine cases out of ten she has not got enough down to convey the intelligence of her mood to any but the most sympathetic and poetical.[39]

Bates recommended that the firm publish the poems, but the selecting, he thought, had not been rigorous enough. He cut the group submitted in half, suggesting to Niles that the remainder would have to be "edited with a good deal of care."[40]

A few more than two hundred poems were submitted to Bates. He numbered all of them, marked with an X those he rejected for publication, and listed his recommendations for Niles by number.[41] Millicent Todd Bingham, in publishing Bates' memorandum to Niles, omitted the list of recommended numbers, explaining that "unfortunately, since his numbering of the poems has not been preserved, those approved or condemned by him cannot, with one or two exceptions, be identified."[42] On the surviving transcripts now in the Amherst College Library, however, there is a series of numbers, scrambled, puzzling, and hitherto unexplained, that match the numbers omitted from Bates' list of recommendations. Marked with an X, the transcripts with these numbers are in fact those submitted to Bates and rejected by him. For example, the number 164 near the top of the transcript reproduced in Figure 1 and the X near the bottom of the same transcript identify the poem "I live with Him—I see His face" (V463) as one chosen by Mrs. Todd and Colonel Higginson for publication in the first series but withdrawn on Bates' advice.[43]

Mrs. Todd and Colonel Higginson did not in every instance follow Bates' advice; together they published several poems that he had rejected. Mrs. Todd claimed to have saved fifteen or twenty, including "I died for Beauty—but was scarce" (V449), "Safe in their Alabaster Chambers" (V216), "Some keep the Sabbath going to Church" (V324), and "How many times these low feet staggered" (V187).[44] Higginson concurred in each instance and on his side indignantly asked how she could let the beautiful "I shall know why—when Time is over" (V193) elude them.[45] In spite of these efforts by the editors, Arlo Bates must be chiefly credited with determining which poems actually appeared in the first series. The selection was first made by Mrs. Todd, then reduced by Colonel Higginson, and then cut in half by Bates. A few poems were included in the first series because the editors overrode Bates' critical judgment, but over ninety of the 116 poems in that volume were included because of his decisions. In the long run, the editors followed Bates' judgment on all but one of his approved poems, while publishing in one or another of the three nineteenth-century volumes about half of those he had banned.

It is not within the scope of this study to examine further Bates' literary judgment. Such a study, however, could now be made by looking closely at the selection of poems in the first series and by examining in detail the poems he is known to have rejected from it (see n. 43). The remaining poems submitted to Bates and rejected by him—some thirty-five—cannot now be identified specifically, but they are among the poems published in the second series (1891).

ALTERING THE POEMS

There is a common misconception that Higginson "itched" to set the crooked straight in Emily Dickinson's poetry and that, as the variorum editor suggests, he was principally responsible for the editorial liberties in the first series.[46] One of the illustrations Mr. Johnson cites is Higginson's insistence on changing the final line of "The Grass so little has to do" (V333): "I wish

I were a Hay." Mrs. Todd wanted to leave the wording of the line as Emily Dickinson wrote it, but Higginson, upset by the unconventional grammar, firmly declared: "It cannot go in so; everybody would say that *hay* is a collective noun requiring the definite article. Nobody can call it *a* hay!"[47] Higginson's insistence on the change, even over Mrs. Todd's objection, would seem to support the belief that he was chiefly responsible for the alterations in the first series. But it should be noted that Mrs. Todd acknowledged that changing "a hay" was the only alteration against which she protested.[48] Moreover, she was herself more than once irritated because Colonel Higginson refused to change Emily Dickinson's ungrammatical use of "lain" for "laid."[49]

The "creative editing" began, according to Mr. Johnson,[50] when Arlo Bates returned the poems with the injunction that changes were "absolutely necessary."[51] But Mrs. Todd's journal account of the editing clearly states that even before the group of poems was submitted to Bates, she had "changed words here and there in the two hundred to make them smoother—he [Colonel Higginson] changed a very few, and put titles to them."[52] The creative editing, then, had begun before Bates saw the poems, with Mrs. Todd apparently changing a good many words to gain smoothness, but with Colonel Higginson changing only "a very few." When the poems did come back from Bates with his injunction, they went, significantly, not to Higginson, but to Mrs. Todd for those "absolutely necessary" changes.[53] It should be clear that the editorial liberties in the first series cannot be ascribed to Higginson alone.

We should not, on the other hand, go to the opposite extreme and entirely free him of responsibility, as one of his biographers has done. Anna Mary Wells in *Dear Preceptor,* her study of Higginson, contends:

> Everyone who has written on this subject, including some very careful and thorough scholars, has said that he regularized rhymes, simplified metaphors, corrected grammar, and smoothed rhythm. It must be a very rash or very

thoroughly convinced biographer who dares to disagree, but the fact is that every surviving word Higginson wrote on this subject for publication or in private letters favored Emily in her "so to speak unregenerate form" [*sic*] against the solid majority that believed she could be improved.[54]

Mrs. Wells' freeing Higginson of all responsibility for alterations is as large a misunderstanding as blaming him too much. Higginson's claim that Emily Dickinson interested him more "in her—so to speak—unregenerate condition" refers to her in 1862 when she first wrote to him for advice; though the claim was made in 1891, it does not refer to his editorial practice.[55] Mrs. Wells believes that all of Higginson's extant writings on the subject of altering Emily Dickinson's poetry are opposed to alterations, but the fact is that when Bates pronounced upon the poems and returned them with the advice that changes were "absolutely necessary," Higginson wrote to Mrs. Todd: "I think Mr. Bates's criticisms excellent. Niles will send you the poems & please revise with these criticisms & then return to me."[56] Mrs. Todd followed his instructions, and a month later, when the poems were in his hands again, he wrote praising her emendation in line 4 of "These are the days when Birds come back" (V130).[57]

Higginson's insistence on changing "a hay" to "the hay" is so well-known that it is curious Mrs. Wells would maintain that he was opposed to such changes. Even so, converting "a hay" into a collective noun was but one of the independent emendations Higginson made in the poems. The famous "Safe in their Alabaster Chambers" (V216) when published in the first series was a composite of two variant versions and had been altered in the second stanza; "I thought it best," Higginson explained to Mrs. Todd, "to combine the two endings on p. 113, with the modification I suggest."[58] On August 26, 1890, he announced changes in two other poems: "On pp. 128, 129, 148 I have made conjectural changes not sustained by MS. Please rub out if you don't approve!"[59] "To know just how He suffered—would be dear" (V622) was the poem on pages 128–29 and was published with two words altered and one added; Mrs. Todd apparently did not approve of Higginson's tinkering with the poem on page 148—"I lost a World—the other day!" (V181)—for it appeared as originally written. Finally, many of the surviving transcripts in the Amherst Collection show editorial changes in Higginson's handwriting that never reached print. Clearly, he was neither wholly innocent nor wholly responsible. Both editors made the rough places plain, and although with only a few exceptions we cannot now determine which editor made a specific alteration in the poems, the responsibility for the editorial liberties was joint.

In the preface to the first series Colonel Higginson declared that the poems were published as written, "with very few and superficial changes."[60] Of the 116 poems that went into this volume, however, over fifty had been changed in various ways. By the editors' conventional standards, Emily Dickinson's poetry frequently had no rhyme or rhythm, and much of the editorial surgery was directed toward giving it some. Words were added or deleted to smooth out lines,[61] and jarring rhymes, such as "balls" paired with "fuse," were adjusted to more soothing patterns, in this case, matching "balls" with "befalls."[62] What gave the editors almost as much trouble as unruly rhymes was Emily Dickinson's penchant for a subjunctive verb form where the indicative normally would have been used. "An Emperor be kneeling," wrote the poet and got it changed by the editors to "is kneeling."[63] Similarly, she frequently left the present, third person singular form of the verb uninflected, as in the line "When Winter shake the Door."[64] In such instances the editors followed standard usage by adding the inflectional s to the verb or by making the subject plural. With the exception of the misuse of "lain" for "laid"—which, curiously enough, Higginson wanted to retain—the editors corrected most elementary lapses in grammar and diction and made the poet's eccentric spelling conform to conventional usage.[65]

Though the editors occasionally disagreed over these changes, their chief difference came over titles to the poems. Higginson had assigned a good many during the winter of 1889–90 when the bundle of transcripts was in his hands. Like Arlo Bates, Mrs. Todd did not care for many of his creations. She thought that some were misleading, and to her mind the Latin ones were pedantic, representing neither the poetry nor Emily Dickinson. She preferred the poems untitled except for the handful that the poet herself had named, but Higginson felt that titles were a necessary aid to the reader. A cordial give-and-take resulted, and the editorial pace was not disrupted. The poems went to Niles on July 14, 1890, and on the thirtieth the first proof came. August and September were devoted to reading proof—Higginson in New Hampshire and Mrs. Todd in Amherst—October to printing and binding. The desire of Lavinia's heart was realized on November 12, 1890, when *Poems by Emily Dickinson* was made public.

RECEPTION OF THE FIRST SERIES

Colonel Higginson had placed an article in the *Christian Union* (September 25, 1890) designed to attract attention to the volume and also to prepare the public for what was coming.[66] But even the article, the titles, and the alterations could not fully disarm criticism. Reviewers were quick to note the "startling disregard of poetic laws."[67] Yet the abuse in the critical notices was usually mixed with acclaim; Arlo Bates reviewed the volume in the same ambivalent terms as in his critique for Niles,[68] and most others concurred: Here was genius dressed in rags. "Madder rhymes," exclaimed Louise Chandler Moulton, "one has seldom seen—scornful disregard of poetic technique could hardly go farther—and yet there is about the book a fascination, a power, a vision that enthralls you, and draws you back to it again and again. Not to have published it would have been a serious loss to the world."[69]

William Dean Howells, anticipating most twentieth-century criticism, took an even bolder stand, claiming that far from being careless or irresponsible the poetry was rough by design:

> Occasionally, the outside of the poem, so to speak, is left so rough, so rude, that the art seems to have faltered. But there is apparent to reflection the fact that the artist

meant just this harsh exterior to remain, and that no grace
of smoothness could have imparted her intention as it
does. . . .

If nothing else had come out of our life but this
strange poetry we should feel that in the work of Emily
Dickinson America, or New England rather, had made a
distinctive addition to the literature of the world, and
could not be left out of any record of it.[70]

Astounded by such unrestrained praise from a critic of Howells'
stature, an English reviewer questioned Howells' seriousness and
charged that Emily Dickinson's effusions were a "farrago of il-
literate and uneducated sentiment . . . as far below the level
of the Poet's Corner in a country newspaper as that is usually
below Shakespeare."[71] Such disparagement was met in America,
too, for her own countrymen, even in their mixed response,
seldom judged her tenderly, Howells being a notable exception.
A year after the first series appeared, the editor of the *Atlantic
Monthly,* Thomas Bailey Aldrich, predicted with apparent satis-
faction that Emily Dickinson was about to be engulfed by
oblivion.[72]

Meanwhile, however, the fame that belonged to Emily Dickinson did not escape her, and commercial success kept Roberts
Brothers more occupied than either Niles or the editors had
anticipated. The first issue of *Poems* was shortly exhausted, and
a second was released on the sixteenth of December. The Christ-
mas demand made another necessary in less than two weeks,
and yet another in January. In spite of the critical quandaries of
reviewers, the public enthusiastically purchased the volume, and
by March 1891 there had been six issues in less than four
months.[73] Niles' severity softened perceptibly, and a second
series was planned on more generous terms than the first had
been. Lavinia, always her sister's keeper, must have felt vindi-
cated.

EDITORIAL PROCEDURE FOR THE
SECOND SERIES

The editorial procedure for the second series was not greatly
unlike that of the first. From the mine of copied poems in her

possession Mrs. Todd extracted over a hundred which she took
to Boston, along with another group which Lavinia requested
be included, to show to Colonel Higginson.[74] There they discussed the new volume, as they had the first one a year and a
half earlier, and the poems were similarly left in Higginson's
hands. But this time he was quick, and since Arlo Bates did not
need to be consulted again, Higginson returned them to Mrs.
Todd for revision just ten days after her visit. He had loosely
classed them under the same four subject heads and had added
Lavinia's choices when they seemed worthy. The arrangement,
he explained, was not to be deemed final, and he promised to
send—and did a few weeks later—copies of poems Emily had
sent to him which should not be omitted. These Mrs. Todd
added to the others and, as she had done previously, performed
the basic editing before she returned them to Higginson. On
July 13, 1891, she sent him the copy arranged, punctuated, and
emended where she thought necessary.[75]

During the work on the second series of poems Colonel Higginson's and Mrs. Todd's attitude toward editorial emendations
showed signs of changing. "Let us alter as little as possible,"
Higginson wrote in April 1891, "now that the public ear is
opened."[76] And three months later when she sent him the copy,
Mrs. Todd was of the opinion that "few changes seem necessary
anywhere."[77] A good many poems in the second series were
altered, however, and once again Anna Mary Wells' biography
of Higginson attempts to place the responsibility upon Mrs.
Todd. As with the first series, Mrs. Wells' view is out of focus.
Maintaining that the editors' correspondence "provides a clear
and fascinating record as to the basic difference in editorial
policy between the two," Mrs. Wells lists four of Mrs. Todd's
changes that are mentioned in the letters. Two of these changes
did not suit Colonel Higginson, and Mrs. Wells concludes that
Mrs. Todd, not he, was the agent of reform in Emily Dickinson's
poetry.[78] But Mrs. Wells fails to mention Higginson's own attempts at change recorded in the editors' correspondence. Puz-
zled by the eighth line of "He put the Belt around my life"

(V273), for example, Higginson suggested an emendation that, in his words, "would be intelligible & rhyme."[79] Mrs. Todd, however, offered an explanation of the line to him and thereby avoided the substitution.[80] And she on her side strongly questioned his changing "One of the ones that Midas touched" (V1466),[81] with Higginson, as a result, agreeing to leave it alone.[82] He made other changes, too, and with some of these Mrs. Todd agreed, as when she wrote with approval of his emendations in " 'The Cricket' [V1068], 'The Battlefield' [V409], etc."[83] (How many more of Higginson's alterations does that "etc." represent?) Nothing except imbalance is to be gained by heaping examples on either editor's half of the scale. Though the editors' attitude toward alterations showed signs of softening, many alterations were made in the second series of poems, and, as with the earlier volume, the responsibility for these alterations was shared by both Mrs. Todd and Colonel Higginson.

CHAPTER II

Midsummer 1891: Manuscript Order and Disorder

When Colonel Higginson received the copy for the second series in July 1891, he worked over Mrs. Todd's punctuation in the poems, reordered her arrangement within subject divisions, and added poems garnered from Emily Dickinson's cousins, Fanny and Lou Norcross. Since time was pressing, the copy did not return to Mrs. Todd, but went directly to Niles to be set in type. Proof would begin arriving in mid-August, and both editors would then be kept busy correcting it, making · last-minute changes, and again struggling over titles.

INDEXING THE MANUSCRIPTS

Meanwhile, between the time of sending the copy to Higginson on July 13 and the arrival of the first proof, Mrs. Todd devoted her efforts to putting the Dickinson manuscripts and her transcripts into manageable order. In her journal she explained how she went about it:

> Before the proof began . . . I made a complete alphabetical index of everything already copied, not including either published volume. This list made nearly one thousand. Then I catalogued the original manuscripts, so that I can find any one at a moment's notice. David helped me a great deal about all this work.[1]

31

At this time the packet poems had been copied and some loose poems too, though the latter had not been approached systematically. Mrs. Todd made a survey of the packets in mid-July to see whether any poems had been omitted in the copying and "found about a dozen—in as many of the little volumes."[2] The transcripts for *Poems* (1890) had been destroyed after publication, and those for the second series she had just sent to Colonel Higginson, but even without the transcripts for the first and second series, she had nearly a thousand to care for. These remaining transcripts she classified according to merit into three groups—A, B, and C—and loosely alphabetized them within each. Keeping the three divisions separate, Mrs. Todd then recorded the first line of every poem in a small leather-covered notebook to which she gave the heading, "Alphabetical list of Emily's poems still unpublished in volumes, July 1891."[3]

The next step was to number all the packets and also the two envelopes in which she kept loose poems that had been copied. The survey in Chapter I of Mrs. Todd's copying showed that the sequence of Todd transcripts (Hammond typewriter, World typewriter, and handwritten) as well as the timing of Miss Graves' employment cannot be reconciled with the numbered order of the packets. The conclusion was that the poems were not copied systematically beginning with packet 1, nor were the packets themselves numbered at the time they were received from Lavinia. Mrs. Todd's journal, quoted above, tells us that after she had prepared the alphabetical list, she then "catalogued the original manuscripts." What can this mean but that during July and August of 1891 she assigned a number to each packet and to the two envelopes? In the margin to the left of each entry in the notebook she then marked the number of the packet or envelope where the original could be found "at a moment's notice."

The transcripts, not the packets, supplied the first lines of the poems for the notebook. Some transcript first lines differ from the corresponding packet lines because Mrs. Todd adopted alternate readings, and when this is the case, the notebook follows the transcript wording. The packet numbers in the notebook, on the other hand, must have come from the packets themselves. It is true that some transcripts have packet numbers written on them and thus could have supplied them for the notebook; such transcripts, however, are few. And though Mrs. Todd, before indexing the poems, may have kept the transcripts in an order corresponding to the packet arrangement, she could not have used this order in recording the numbers in the notebook, since the order had been destroyed when she classified and alphabetized the transcripts. Instead she went through the packets poem by poem marking the packet number next to the appropriate entry in the notebook.

Understanding precisely how Mrs. Todd went about indexing the poems is requisite to putting the manuscripts in proper order. In 1950 when Harvard University came into possession of packets 1–40, many of them had been cut up and disarranged. The leather-covered notebook can be the key to putting them in their proper order since an analysis of its entries will reveal the arrangement of the manuscripts upon which it was based. If the packet numbers in the notebook had come from the transcripts, the notebook might have reflected the state of the manuscripts at the time of copying or shortly thereafter, but since the numbers came directly from the packets themselves, the notebook is the key to the order of the packets as they stood in July–August 1891 when Mrs. Todd went through them.

This fact about the notebook can help establish when the mutilation of the manuscripts took place. The notebook identifies the packet location for six poems cut out of four of the mutilated packets.* Emily Dickinson's holographs for these are now lost, but Mrs. Todd's transcripts survive, providing our only source for the poems. Since these transcripts did not supply the packet numbers in the notebook, it is clear that the packets suffered mutilation sometime after July–August 1891 because they had to be intact then in order for Mrs. Todd to record the proper number next to the notebook entry.

* See below, pp. 46–48.

Suspicion that Mrs. Todd may have participated in the mutilation should be dispelled by a comparison of the packets at Harvard with those at Amherst College. The former, numbered 1–40, were returned to Lavinia and thereafter were in the possession of Susan Dickinson, her daughter Martha Dickinson Bianchi, and finally Mrs. Bianchi's friend Alfred Leete Hampson. These manuscripts have been shuffled, cut up, and generally dealt with roughly. The others, numbered 80–95, along with many loose poems, remained with Mrs. Todd and passed afterwards into the possession of her daughter, Millicent Todd Bingham, who gave them to Amherst College. These packets are in good order. They have not been mutilated, and, significantly, the notebook does not indicate that any poems are missing from them.[4]

THE MANUSCRIPTS

The introduction to the variorum provides the following description of the manuscripts:

> With a blue pencil Professor Todd placed a number at the top of the first page of each packet and, as they later came into his house, on the envelopes containing the remaining manuscripts. His sequence goes 1 through 40, 80 through 110. A tabulation shows that numbers 1–40, 80–83 are all threaded packets, that numbers 84–98 are packets of loose sheets prepared as if for threading. Beyond that point the grouping is miscellaneous, with no discoverable sequence except as the arrangements reflect Mrs. Todd's effort to produce a semblance of order among manuscripts that had in fact no order at all.[5]

The questions of who numbered the manuscripts and when the numbering was done have already been touched upon, but a few other comments are necessary here, for the description is inaccurate. First, the "scraps"—loose poems frequently on odds and ends of paper—came to Mrs. Todd not in envelopes, but in a box or boxes, as her letters and private papers testify. The envelopes were an editorial necessity designed, as Mr. Johnson suggests, "to produce a semblance of order among manuscripts that had in fact no order at all." Though Mrs. Todd had hardly begun to copy the scraps when she ceased working on the Dickinson manuscripts, she did provide the envelopes for them, numbering two of the envelopes (97 and 98) and including these two in the notebook listing. The other envelopes (96, 99–110) were not included in it and were numbered by Millicent Todd Bingham in the present century.

The description of the manuscripts quoted above lists envelopes 96–98 as being among the "packets of loose sheets prepared as if for threading." But these three envelopes, as well as those numbered 99–110, cannot truly be called "packets" if that term is to be synonymous with fascicle. The poems Emily Dickinson bound into fascicles had been carefully copied on sheets of stationery generally of uniform size. The poems in the envelopes frequently were on odd-shaped scraps of paper— everything from newspaper clippings to brown paper sacks— that the poet used when jotting down her sudden inspiration. They were arbitrarily gathered into the envelopes by Mrs. Todd and give no evidence of having been "prepared as if for threading."[6]

Although the variorum indicates that the threaded packets run consecutively from 1 to 40 and from 80 to 83, examination shows that 84 and 85 were also threaded and in fact still are.[7] Thus the unthreaded packets begin at 86, and, since the envelopes 96–98 cannot be called packets, they stop at 95. Though the kind and size of paper vary at times within these unthreaded packets, they are not gatherings of odds and ends upon which Emily Dickinson composed. The poems in packets 86–95 are on sheets of stationery, neatly copied, but not threaded, though they do seem as if they had been gathered together for threading. It should also be noted that the packets at Harvard numbered 33, 35, 36, and 38 were likewise not threaded. These have been bound with a single brass fastener each. They resemble the unthreaded packets 86–95 in that the paper, handwriting, and ink vary at times from sheet to sheet, and like 86–95, they were probably unbound packets. There are no other instances of Emily Dickinson's using brass fasteners for binding, and those in packets 33, 35, 36, and 38 were most likely inserted by another hand than hers in order to keep the loose sheets together.[8]

In summary: Mrs. Todd provided the envelopes used to house the scraps and other loose poems. She numbered envelopes 97 and 98 and included them in the notebook inventory; Mrs. Bingham numbered the others. The threaded packets—those bound by Emily Dickinson herself—are 1–32, 34, 37, 39–40, and 80–85. Between these two manuscript states there is a third—those which Emily Dickinson copied from the scraps, but which she did not bind—forming a kind of proto-packet. The numbers of these are 33, 35, 36, 38, and 86–95. We should not be disturbed by the disorderly sequence of numbers within each category, since the numbering of the manuscripts was an arbitrary arrangement by Mrs. Todd that represents neither stages in the editorial copying nor stages in Emily Dickinson's creative process.[9]

One must agree with the variorum editor that "there is no ready explanation" why the numbering of the packets stopped at 40 and began again at 80.[10] The 1891 notebook itself confirms this division, for it has no numbers 41–79. Since the break in numbering might suggest that manuscripts are missing, Mr. Johnson, in the introduction to the variorum, discusses why that is not the case. His contention that the break does not represent lost manuscripts is surely correct, but the proof is faulty. He explains that

> The record book survives wherein Mrs. Todd listed the first lines of all poems she knew about, except the worksheet drafts which comprise envelopes 99–110. This list, together with the poems in the final twelve envelopes, establishes the total of all poems known to have been among Emily Dickinson's papers at the time of her death.[11]

Mr. Johnson's explanation, however, overlooks the fact that, as we have seen, the indexing done in midsummer 1891 omitted

from the notebook nearly three hundred poems that were published in the first and second series. Moreover, the notebook
does not include the few poems in envelope 96.

As further proof that the break in the numbering does not
represent lost manuscripts, Mr. Johnson cites Mrs. Todd's
statement that the box of threaded "volumes" contained "eight
or nine hundred poems tied up in this way" and then adds the
number of poems in packets 1–40 and 80–83, arriving at a
total of "exactly 879."[12] Yet four of the packets whose poems
are included in this total are not threaded, but bound with brass
fasteners, while two threaded packets are omitted. Moreover,
the figure here differs from that in Appendix 6 of the variorum,
where the total for the same packets is 844.[13] Either figure, of
course, comes reasonably close to Mrs. Todd's estimate of "eight
or nine hundred poems," but even so, the argument is faulty,
for Mrs. Todd's estimate was supposedly based on "over sixty
little 'volumes,' "[14] while Mr. Johnson's figures cover only a
few over forty. Indeed Mrs. Todd's statement would seem to
indicate lost fascicles; she made her statement, however, forty-
five years after she first saw the manuscripts, and on this subject
her memory did not have long-distance accuracy: her estimate
in 1932 was "eight or nine hundred poems";[15] in 1930 it was
600,[16] while in 1890–91 she and Lavinia said 700.[17] But the
conclusion that the break in numbering between 40 and 80 does
not represent lost manuscripts is correct. The proof is simple:
Mrs. Todd listed in her notebook poems from all the packets
that she knew about, and there are no packet numbers in the
notebook between 40 and 80.

THE HOUGHTON COLLECTION
AND THE NOTEBOOK

It is difficult to explain why the gap between 40 and 80,
already there in 1891, should mark the division in manuscripts
between those Lavinia had and those Mrs. Todd retained, since
the split between the women did not come until 1896. But that
is the way the manuscripts divided. When the Houghton Library

acquired Lavinia's share, then augmented with others the poet had sent to her sister-in-law, Susan Dickinson, and to Sue's family, a member of the staff numbered the sheets in the order they were in when received, and an inventory was prepared. Later it was discovered that this order was false, and on the basis of sewing holes, paper, and handwriting, Mr. Johnson with the help of two associates switched sheets between several packets and also incorporated a few of the loose sheets into them. The result, the present arrangement at the Houghton Library, was completed in 1952 and formed the basis for the variorum description of the manuscripts.

The Houghton arrangement is a curious grouping even at quick glance. Mr. Johnson believes that the packets were numbered in blue pencil on the first sheet as Lavinia brought them to the Todds, yet in the arrangement at Houghton the sheet marked 28 is located in packet 5, and the sheet marked 24 may be found in packet 39. Moreover, packet 10 contains only one poem on one sheet, which hardly satisfies the poet's motive for having a packet.[18] Mr. Johnson has aptly remarked that "there can be no assurance that the packets . . . are in fact today grouped as Emily Dickinson originally assembled them."[19]

Mrs. Todd's notebook, however, can assist us toward a nearly complete reconstruction of Emily Dickinson's groupings despite the fact that nearly three hundred poems are not included in it. Emily Dickinson copied her poems, one after another, onto sheets of stationery until the sheets were full. If the notebook identifies the packet location for one or more poems on a given sheet, then the packet location for the rest of the poems on that sheet is also established even though these poems are not listed in the notebook. In working with the notebook, then, the unit is not the poem, but the sheet. In the original Houghton inventory the sheets that comprise the packets were numbered consecutively from 1 to 219.[20] The notebook indicates the packet placement of all except ten of them.[21] Three of these exceptions can be placed with some confidence since they are the first sheets of their respective packets and display the packet number penciled in blue.[22] Most sheets so numbered go into the packet cor-responding to their number, and there is no particular reason to consider these as exceptions. Six other sheets that the notebook does not identify must be placed on the basis of sewing holes, paper, and handwriting.[23] They fortunately offer no great dif-ficulty. In each case the original Houghton inventory and the variorum agree as to their placement. I have double-checked them and see no reason to suspect they might be misplaced.

Every poem on the nine sheets discussed in the preceding paragraph was published in either the first or the second series, which is the reason they are not represented in the notebook. Mrs. Todd has, however, left another record that supports the present placement. On the list she made of the contents of the second series[24] she marked the packet source for the poems in that volume. Eight of the nine sheets here considered are thus placed precisely where they are now. The ninth, H 195, was published in the first series and consequently is represented neither in the notebook nor on this list. H 195, however, has no appearance of being misplaced and need not occupy us longer.

The tenth and final sheet that is not represented in the note-book properly goes into packet 29, but its placement is more difficult to determine than that of the preceding nine. Sheet H 70, found in packet 14 at the time of the Houghton inventory, contains three poems published in either the first or second series (and therefore not listed in the notebook) and a fourth poem, unpublished in either series, "My Reward for Being—was This" (V343). Emily Dickinson wrote two versions of this poem and copied one onto a sheet in packet 6 and the other onto H 70. Miss Graves made a transcript of the latter version.[25] Mrs. Todd herself made the transcript of the variant version in packet 6,[26] and she entered the poem's first line in the record book. Since the only packet number next to this entry is 6, the notebook cannot help us place sheet H 70. It must be placed from other evidence.

The other evidence is contradictory. Mrs. Todd's list of the contents of the second series has the packet number *14* next to a poem that comes from H 70 ("God made a little Gentian").[27] Yet this packet location for the sheet is unconvincing. H 70 is an obvious alien in packet 14, for the necessary correspondences are lacking. The sheet is cream stationery, lightly ruled, and embossed with a crest (enclosing a double-headed eagle) that is surmounted by the letters *WM*. The paper in packet 29 is identical, while packet 14 has no similar sheets. The handwriting also matches packet 29 (all 1862 according to the variorum), but, more important, the sewing holes fit exactly; packet 14 meets neither of these tests. Furthermore, Miss Graves was the copyist for packet 29 as well as for H 70, but she copied nothing from packet 14. Finally, the notebook identifies V1712 ("A Pit —but Heaven over it") as one of the missing poems from packet 29.* The transcript for it is Miss Graves' (as one would expect),[28] but on the verso Mrs. Todd made notations of other poems in packet 29, one of which was "God made a little Gentian"—from H 70. It is clear, then, that this sheet belongs to packet 29, that it was there when Miss Graves copied the packet in 1889, but that between then and midsummer 1891 the sheet was misplaced in packet 14, where it was resting when Mrs. Todd made her list of the contents of the second series and where it remained until Mr. Johnson transferred it back to packet 29.

The Placement of H 157

Packet 29 presents an additional problem. According to Mr. Johnson, sheet H 157 (Fig. 6) in this packet forms the conclusion to "I tie my Hat—I crease my Shawl" (V443), which is on sheet H 19 and was found in packet 5 when it was inventoried at the Houghton Library.[29] On the basis of manuscript evidence he argued sheet H 19 out of packet 5 and into 29. The notebook supports his transfer, but the problem is not so easily resolved. "I tie my Hat" is the first of the two poems on H 19 and occupies both sides of the first leaf. To conclude this poem, H 157 would have to go inside the fold of sheet 19. But

---

* See below, pp. 46–47.

'T would start them -
As - could tremolo -
But - since we got - a
Bomb.
And held it in our Bosom.
Nay - Hold it - it is Calm -

Therefore - As do Life's
Cabn.
Though Life's Reward - be done -
With scrupulous exactness.
To hold our Senses - on.

the sewing holes of H 157, which indeed perfectly fit those of packet 29, cannot be aligned properly when placed inside this fold. They do not in fact show at all. Emily Dickinson clearly never bound the sheets in the order that the variorum suggests.

As corroborative evidence for linking "I tie my Hat" and H 157, Mr. Johnson cites the fact that

> Mrs. Bingham published the last nine lines [H 157], arranged as two quatrains, as the two final stanzas of "I tie my Hat," in *New England Quarterly,* XX (1947), 34–35, from a transcript made by her mother. Thus at the time Mrs. Todd saw the manuscript, the two sheets were in their correct order in packet 29.[30]

Mr. Johnson's reasoning assumes that Mrs. Todd was the copyist for "I tie my Hat" and that in copying the poem she also included the lines from H 157. The transcript, however, was not made by Mrs. Todd, but by Miss Graves, and all Miss Graves copied was the twenty-four lines on sheet 19 that constitute "I tie my Hat."[31] If H 19 and H 157 had been associated in the manner Mr. Johnson suggests, Miss Graves would have copied them as a whole. Instead she made a separate transcript for each of the stanzas on H 157, as might be expected, since both stanzas are followed by a drawn line, usually Emily Dickinson's signal for the end of a poem.

Nevertheless, sheet 157, like sheet 19, does belong to packet 29, as manuscript evidence and a notebook entry prove.[32] It is likely that the packet had already become untied when Mrs. Todd saw it, for she too was confused by the two verses on H 157 as well as by "I tie my Hat" itself. At the end of the Graves transcript, from which Mrs. Bingham published the poem, Mrs. Todd copied the extra two stanzas, but next to the second stanza she added the query, "Is this a part of it?" In the manuscript "I tie my Hat" is divided with twelve lines on the first page and lines 13–24 on the verso. Not sure how many poems were intended, Mrs. Todd has at the end of line 12 in Miss Graves' transcript written the question, "Is this another?" —meaning, Does the next line begin another poem? Further indication of her uncertainty about H 157 and "I tie my Hat" is the fact that she made an independent transcript of "There-fore—we do life's labor" from H 157 and also made a separate copy of lines 13–24 of "I tie my Hat" but did not add either stanza from H 157 to it. In the 1891 notebook she ranked the Graves transcript of "I tie my Hat" as a *B* poem while each of the other stanzas was separately classed as a *C*. The conclusion is inevitable: Mrs. Todd did not know how the sheets were to be arranged. Emily Dickinson, as we have seen, could not have bound them in the order the variorum now has them, and its printing of "I tie my Hat" is incorrect. The last nine lines should be removed from the poem.

Where then do they go? Though difficult, this question is an-swerable. The verso of H 157 is blank; the two stanzas on the recto are reproduced in Figure 6. The paper, handwriting, and sewing holes correspond exactly with the rest of packet 29, and it might be thought that these two stanzas are separate poems, belonging to packet 29, since both are followed by the line that usually marks the end of a poem in the packets. But Emily Dickinson did not commonly copy two small poems like these and then leave two-thirds of the available space empty. Besides, strictly speaking, H 157 is not a sheet at all, but only a half sheet separated at the fold from the rest. The poet apparently used this half sheet to add stanzas to one of the other poems in packet 29. When the sheet was bound in the packet, it was outside, not inside, the regular folded sheets of stationery and therefore must have been intended as an addition to one of the poems coming last on those sheets.

The final poems on the sheets in packet 29 are "A still—Volcano—Life" (V601), "It feels a shame to be Alive" (V444), "My Reward for Being—was This" (V343), "The Spider holds a Silver Ball" (V605), "It always felt to me—a wrong" (V597), and one, but not both, of the two poems now missing from the packet: "A curious Cloud surprised the Sky" (V1710) or "A Pit—but Heaven over it" (V1712).* Manu-

* See below, pp. 46–47.

script appearance and/or poetic sense rule out all but "A still—Volcano—Life" and "A Pit—but Heaven over it." The first is the poem to which the poet's niece, Martha Dickinson Bianchi, attached the second stanza on H 157 when she published it in *Further Poems* (1929).[33] Thomas Johnson says that she unaccountably omitted the first stanza on H 157,[34] but her doing so is actually quite understandable: each of the two stanzas on H 157 is followed by Emily Dickinson's line, suggesting that each is a separate unit and that they are not to be joined as one. To Mrs. Bianchi, the stanzas presented a choice of one stanza or the other.

Either of the two stanzas might seem to be an appropriate addition to the poem "A still—Volcano—Life" (V601). This poem deals with life in terms of dormant volcanic activity and an accompanying earthquake that is "Too subtle to suspect / By natures this side Naples." "The North," the poet explains, "cannot detect / The Solemn—Torrid—Symbol." The first stanza on H 157—

> 'Twould start them—
> We—could tremble—
> But since we got a Bomb—
> And held it in our Bosom—
> Nay—Hold it—it is calm—

might seem to be an addition to "A still—Volcano—Life" in which "them" (line 1) refers to the people of the North and "tremble" (line 2) is part of the earthquake metaphor. The gist of the second stanza on H 157 is that we do life's labor with "scrupulous exactness" in order to steady our senses in the midst of life's terrors. When Mrs. Bianchi put this stanza at the end of the poem in *Further Poems,* she apparently saw it as a conclusion to the volcano and earthquake descriptions that then preceded it.

Yet in comparison to "A Pit—but Heaven over it" (V1712) Mrs. Bianchi's choice seems inappropriate. The second stanza on H 157 points out the need to steady ourselves in the midst of life's terrors, yet in the poem to which Mrs. Bianchi attached it the volcano is still (line 1) and the earthquake style is quiet (line 5). V1712, on the other hand, treats terrors openly:

> A Pit—but Heaven over it—
> And Heaven beside, and Heaven abroad;
> And yet a Pit—
> With Heaven over it.
>
> To stir would be to slip—   5
> To look would be to drop—
> To dream—to sap the Prop
> That holds my chances up.
> Ah! Pit! With Heaven over it!
>
> The depth is all my thought—   10
> I dare not ask my feet—
> 'Twould start us where we sit
> So straight you'd scarce suspect
> It was a Pit—with fathoms under it
> Its Circuit just the same   15
> Seed—summer—tomb—
> Whose Doom to whom

Certainly the second stanza on H 157 follows more appropriately from the terrors of this pit than from the still volcano and quiet earthquake of the poem to which Mrs. Bianchi attached it.

At the same time, the first stanza on H 157 seems written specifically for "A Pit—but Heaven over it." I quote the stanza again:

> 'Twould start them—
> We—could tremble—
> But since we got a Bomb—
> And held it in our Bosom—
> Nay—Hold it—it is calm—

This five-line stanza does not fit easily into the unbroken regularity of quatrains in the other eligible poems in packet 29, but the irregularity of "A Pit" accommodates it readily. Notice the parallel between " 'Twould start us where we sit" (line 12) and " 'Twould start them" (the first line on H 157). Notice too the visual repetition in "tomb" (line 16) and "Bomb" (the third line on H 157) as well as the extended repetition of the *m* sound starting with line 16 in the poem and continuing through the final line of the stanza from H 157. (Earlier in the poem the poet had similarly exploited *t* and *p*.) The holograph for "A Pit" is now lost, so that the version quoted above comes from Miss Graves' transcript.[35] It seems to end abruptly in the middle of a thought. If the stanza on H 157 is added, however, the thought continues unbroken: "Whose Doom to whom / 'Twould start them."[36]

The first five lines on H 157, then, do not form a stanza by themselves, but are the continuation of "A Pit." The poem was too long for Emily Dickinson to copy complete on the folded sheet. H 157 was her means of accommodating the overflow. The other lines on H 157—

> Therefore—we do life's labor—
> Though life's Reward—be done—
> With scrupulous exactness—
> To hold our Senses—on—

must then be either alternate lines or a conclusion to the whole poem. The former was most likely the poet's intention. If she had intended these four lines as a conclusion, there would have been no need for her to separate them from the rest of the poem with the line that she drew (see Fig. 6). Such a line probably indicates that she considered the poem to terminate at that point and that the remaining four lines on the sheet form an alternate for the final four lines in the poem.

The Placement of Missing Poems

The notebook Mrs. Todd used for indexing the poems in midsummer 1891 shows that twenty-five of the forty packets at the Houghton Library are now constituted as they were then: packets 1–4, 6–7, 9, 12, 15, 18–22, 25, 27, 30–35, 37–38, and 40. Five others would be so assembled except that, generally as the result of mutilation, parts of them are missing. The notebook places the following six poems in four of these five packets:

Packet 8—V1737: "Rearrange a 'Wife's' affection!"
Packet 13—V1725: "I took one Draught of Life"

Packet 16—V1727: "If ever the lid gets off my head"
          V1739: "Some say goodnight—at night"
Packet 29—V1710: "A curious Cloud surprised the Sky"
          V1712: "A Pit—but Heaven over it"

Lacking holograph copies for these poems, we must rely on transcripts made by Mrs. Todd and Miss Graves for our textual source. These transcripts, however, do not enable us to date the poems, and Mr. Johnson published them in the final section of the variorum where they are arranged alphabetically, not chronologically. When the missing poems are associated with their packets, however, they can be dated with fair certainty, since all of the poems within any one of these particular packets are of the same period. According to the variorum chronology, Emily Dickinson copied the one into packet 8 sometime in 1861, and the five belonging to packets 13, 16, and 29 were done the year following.[37]

Within each of these packets the stationery is likewise uniform, allowing us to anticipate the appearance of the absent pieces. We may even predict, on the basis of manuscript appearance, that the poem missing from packet 13 was on the missing first leaf of H 62, that those in packet 16 were on the missing first leaf of H 89, and that those in packet 29 were on the missing second leaf of H 155. The first leaf of H 62 was also the first in the packet when it was numbered and, if found, should display a *13* marked on it in blue pencil. In all likelihood, "I took one Draught of Life" will not be the only poem there, since it is only two quatrains in length and there would be room for as many as eight quatrains. What poems could be missing from the packets and also not identified in the 1891 notebook? Only those that were published in the first or second series and thus not listed in the notebook. This narrows the visible choice, according to Appendix 11 of the variorum ("Distribution of Missing Autographs"), to two poems: "A train went through a burial gate" (V1761) and "My country need not change her gown" (V1511).[38] Each poem is two quatrains in length, and either one or both may have filled part of the remaining space on the leaf from packet 13.[39]

The fifth of the packets in which the 1891 notebook places a poem not presently there is packet 36. "I worked for chaff and earning Wheat" (V1269) was part of that packet in 1891. Unlike the poems missing from the other packets, a manuscript of this one is extant and, as it turns out, is the missing part itself. Packet 36 was not threaded, but was bound with a brass fastener, and the slit where the prongs pierced the manuscripts comes 3⅝ inches from the top edge of the sheets and ¼ inch from the left edge. A copy of "I worked for chaff" that was among Mrs. Todd's papers at her death has within recent years been given by Millicent Todd Bingham to the Library of Congress. The manuscript is now laminated, but the slit where the fastener pierced it can be discerned and comes 3⅝ inches from the top edge of the sheet and ¼ inch from the left edge. The Library of Congress manuscript of this poem clearly belongs to packet 36 at the Houghton Library.[40]

Reordering Packets 39, 24, and 11

If the seven missing poems whose placement has just been discussed were now associated with their respective packets at the Houghton Library, thirty of the forty packets there would be assembled as they were when Mrs. Todd cataloged them in midsummer 1891 (packets 1–4, 6–9, 12–13, 15–16, 18–22, 25, 27, 29–38, and 40). Twenty-one of the thirty packets were received at the Houghton Library in this condition. With the exception of the missing poems, Mr. Johnson put the other nine in their 1891 order: packets 6, 8, 13, 16, 21, 29, 32, 36, and 38. It was no easy task. In just these nine, one sheet was shifted, five sheets were removed, and six added from other packets.[41] Mr. Johnson also looked among the loose poems, whose numbering begins at 220, and brought seven back into the fold. H 220 he placed in packet 8 and H 281 in packet 36, while the five sheets numbered 380–84 went into packets 38, 6, 5, 29, and 16 respectively. The notebook confirms Mr. Johnson's detective work in every case, including the assigning of H 382 to packet 5. This packet, it will be noted, is not included in the list of thirty, for in spite of the addition of H 382, packet 5 is still not assembled as it was in midsummer 1891. It is but one of ten packets at the Houghton Library that are not. Three of these packets will be discussed in this section, then three in the section that follows. The remaining four (packets 10, 14, 23, and 26)—improperly assembled even in 1891—will be discussed later in this chapter after four other packets (2, 3, 6, and 27), also improperly assembled in 1891, have been considered.

Mrs. Todd's notebook indicates that the six sheets now forming packet 39 belong to packet 24.[42] This is not surprising since the first sheet is numbered 24 in blue pencil and the remaining five sheets match it perfectly in regard to paper, handwriting, and sewing holes. Strictly speaking, the packet is assembled properly, but is labeled incorrectly. Each of the poems in the variorum attributed to packet 39 is actually from packet 24.[43] But packet 24 currently has three sheets of its own, H 131–33, that do not correspond in the necessary ways with the sheets we are importing from packet 39. These three, which are cream, lightly ruled, and faintly embossed with a capitol, must be part of another grouping. Their mates turn up in packet 11: three sheets numbered H 50–52.

The sewing holes of the two sets match, though on H 50–52 they have been ripped through the folded edge, while on H 131–33 the holes are not torn. In the introduction to the variorum the editor stressed that in his transfer of manuscripts he took into account not only corresponding spacing in thread holes, but also identical shape in tears.[44] The difference in tears in the present instance may have prevented him from linking the two sets of sheets, but if so, it was a misleading scruple. Once a sheet has been made to fit elsewhere than in its original packet, it will thereafter always fit two places, and it will be extremely difficult to tell whether the shape of the tear identifies its original position or was acquired in some subsequent gathering. Not only the paper but the ink is identical for these six sheets, and Emily Dickinson's handwriting appears to be of the same vintage, even though Mr. Johnson assigned the sets to different years, H 50–52 to 1862 and H 131–33 to 1863. Despite the difference in tears and the discrepancy in the variorum dating, quite probably erroneous, the sheets do go together—as evidenced also by the fact that thirteen of the seventeen poems covering the six sheets are recorded in the 1891 notebook and next to each Mrs. Todd entered an *11*. Packet 11, then, should be assembled as shown in Table 4. The asterisks denote the transferred sheets for which the variorum description needs correction.

PACKET 11

Sheet	Poem	
H 50a	Bereavement in their death to feel	V645
b	I think To Live—may be a Bliss	V646
c	A little Road—not made of Man—	V647
H 51a	Promise This—When You be Dying—	V648
b	I had no time to Hate—	V478
H 52a	Her Sweet turn to leave the Homestead	V649
b	Pain—has an Element of Blank—	V650
c	So much Summer	V651
*H 131a	My Life had stood—a Loaded Gun—	V754
b	The Sunrise runs for Both—	V710
c	No Bobolink—reverse His Singing	V755
*H 132a	One Blessing had I than the rest	V756
b	Victory comes late—	V690
c	The Mountains—grow unnoticed—	V757
*H 133a	These—saw Visions—	V758
b	Strong Draughts of Their Refreshing Minds	V711
c	We miss Her—not because We see—	V993
d	Essential Oils—are wrung—	V675

Table 4.—Proposed revision of packet 11. The sheets with an asterisk are transfers from packet 24.

But if the correct order of packets 24 and 11 has now been restored, what of packet 39? The answer is that there is no packet 39, nor was there one in midsummer 1891. Mr. Johnson has explained that the "numbers set down in the record book exactly correspond with the evidence of the packets: they range from 1 to 40, and from 80 to 98."[45] That is their range, but there is no entry in the entire notebook for a packet 39. Accommodating such a packet led to the misplacement of manuscripts.[46]

Reordering Packets 28, 5, and 17

Packets 28, 5, and 17 also need to be rearranged. They are complicated because the paper of all three is the same (with or without LEE MASS embossed) and because Emily Dickinson wrote out the poems in the same year, 1862. Thus manuscript evidence is restricted to sewing holes, which can be deceptive. When it was inventoried at the Houghton Library, packet 28

PACKET 28

Sheet	Poem	
*H 149a	From Cocoon forth a Butterfly	V354
b	Her sweet Weight on my Heart a Night	V518
c	'Tis Opposites—entice—	V355
*H 150a	The Day that I was crowned	V356
b	'Twas warm—at first—like Us—	V519
c	God is a distant—stately Lover—	V357
d	If any sink, assure that this, now standing—	V358
H 151a	The Night was wide, and furnished scant	V589
b	To love thee Year by Year—	V434
c	Did you ever stand in a Cavern's Mouth—	V590
d	Much Madness is divinest Sense—	V435
H 152a	The Wind—tapped like a tired Man—	V436
b	To interrupt His Yellow Plan	V591
c	Prayer is the little implement	V437
H 153a	What care the Dead, for Chanticleer—	V592
b	Forget! The lady with the Amulet	V438
c	Undue Significance a starving man attaches	V439
H 154a	I think I was enchanted	V593
b	'Tis customary as we part	V440
c	The Battle fought between the Soul	V594

Table 5.—Proposed revision of packet 28. The sheets with an asterisk are transfers from packet 5.

contained sheets 149–54. Mr. Johnson removed the first two and placed them in packet 5, where they still are, even though the first is marked with the blue pencil 28. This was probably done because of a similarity in the rip of the sewing holes on these sheets and on those he has in packet 5. And indeed the two sets of sheets may have been bound together at one time. But the sewing holes of H 149–50 perfectly match the sewing holes of the other sheets in packet 28, and, as the notebook indicates, these sheets do in fact belong with the ones there.[47] Table 5 shows the correct assembly of packet 28.

PACKET 5

Sheet	Poem	
H 18a	No Crowd that has occurred	V515
b	Beauty—be not caused—It Is—	V516
c	He parts Himself—like Leaves—	V517
*H 91a	'Tis true—They shut me in the Cold—	V538
b	The Province of the Saved	V539
c	I took my Power in my Hand—	V540
d	Some such Butterfly be seen	V541
*H 93a	I had no Cause to be awake—	V542
b	I fear a Man of frugal Speech—	V543
c	Rehearsal to Ourselves	V379
d	The Martyr Poets—did not tell—	V544
*H 95a	I cross till I am weary	V550
b	Answer July—	V386
c	There is a Shame of Nobleness—	V551
*H 96a	An ignorance a Sunset	V552
b	One Crucifixion is recorded—only—	V553
c	The Sweetest Heresy recieved	V387
d	Take Your Heaven further on—	V388
H 382a	I started Early—Took my Dog—	V520
b	"Morning"—means "Milking"—to the Farmer—	V300
c	Endow the Living—with the Tears—	V521

Table 6.—Proposed revision of packet 5. Sheets H 149–50 are transfers to packet 28, H 20 and 22 to packet 17. The sheets marked with an asterisk are transfers from packet 17.

Packet 5, however, is also involved in a mix-up with packet 17 that misplaces six sheets. The assortment of sheets now comprising packet 5 at the Houghton Library can be made to fit each other only by an inordinate amount of fiddling, and then neither the top nor the bottom trim edges are evenly adjusted. All will be straight if sheets 20 and 22 go to packet 17 from packet 5 and sheets 91, 93, 95, and 96 are brought back in exchange. The notebook supports these shifts with many entries. This proposed rearrangement of packets 5, 17, and 28 is also

PACKET 17

Sheet	Poem	
H 90a	The Soul's Superior instants	V306
b	Me prove it now—Whoever doubt	V537
c	To lose one's faith—surpass	V377
d	I saw no Way—The Heavens were stitched—	V378
H 94a	There is a flower that Bees prefer—	V380
b	A Secret told—	V381
c	For Death—or rather	V382
H 67a	Exhiliration—is within—	V383
b	'Tis One by One—the Father counts—	V545
c	To fill a Gap	V546
d	I've seen a Dying Eye	V547
H 68a	No Rack can torture me—	V384
b	Death is potential to that Man	V548
c	Smiling back from Coronation	V385
d	That I did always love	V549
*H 20a	The Future never spoke—	V672
b	I gained it so—	V359
c	Death sets a Thing significant	V360
d	What I can do—I will—	V361
*H 22a	Had I presumed to hope—	V522
b	Sweet—You forgot—but I remembered	V523
c	It struck me—every Day—	V362
d	I went to thank Her—	V363

Table 7.—Proposed revision of packet 17. Sheets H 91, 93, 95, 96 are transfers to packet 5. The sheets marked with an asterisk are transfers from packet 5.

supported by the transcript patterns for these packets when they are so arranged: packet 5 (Table 6) was copied entirely by Miss Graves, packet 17 (Table 7) was done on the Hammond typewriter with black ribbon, while packet 28 (Table 5) was copied by Mrs. Todd by hand.

Reordering Packets 2 and 3, 6 and 27

The preceding discussions have marshaled three kinds of evidence to support the proposed rearrangements: (1) the 1891 notebook, (2) transcript patterns, and (3) the characteristics of the paper, sewing holes, ink, and handwriting of the manuscripts. Each represents a different date in the history of the manuscripts bound in fascicles: the first describes the order at the time of indexing in midsummer 1891; the second reflects the order when the poems were copied during 1887–89; and the third indicates the arrangement in which Emily Dickinson bound them between 1858 and her death in 1886. For packets 11, 24, and the non-existent 39, and packets 5, 17, and 28, the three kinds of evidence are in agreement as to the order of the manuscripts. In other words, these fascicles were in the same order when copied and indexed as they were when Emily Dickinson first bound them. The displacement of sheets occurred after midsummer 1891.

In other instances displacement occurred before 1891, and in such cases the three kinds of evidence will not be in agreement. In attempting to arrange the fascicles as Emily Dickinson had them, an editor, if possible, should not rely on any of the evidence exclusively, since sewing holes can be deceptive and since the transcript patterns and the 1891 inventory represent the order of the manuscripts several years after the poet bound them. But if there is disagreement in the three kinds of evidence, priority must be given to the manuscript evidence, since it alone reflects Emily Dickinson's own order.

The three kinds of evidence disagree about the placement of the sheets in packets 2 and 3. The notebook places sheets 5–8 in packet 2 and sheets 9–12 in packet 3. But the transcript pattern for packet 2 (see Table 2) contradicts the notebook order. The Hammond typewriter was Mrs. Todd's first mode of copying, the World machine was the second; yet the first sheet in this gathering was copied with the second machine and the remaining were copied with the first. One should suspect that the packet is not in the order in which it was copied, and in fact it is not. Sheet 5 at that time was with sheets 9–12 in packet 3, and all were copied on the World machine on paper Y. Manuscript evidence proposes another, earlier arrangement for the sheets in packets 2 and 3. The paper, ink, and handwriting match exactly, and the sewing holes are identical, indicating that Emily Dickinson bound all the sheets now classed as packets 2 and 3 into one gathering. Later these sheets became separated, were then transcribed in a new order, and indexed in 1891 in yet another.

Packets 6 and 27 were similarly disordered sometime after Emily Dickinson bound them and before Mrs. Todd indexed them. Originally packet 27 was composed of eight sheets: H 144–48, H 23–24, and H 73. By the time of copying, the last three of these sheets had been removed and were copied separately from the others. Miss Graves was copyist for H 144–48, while Mrs. Todd made Hammond typescripts of H 23–24 and handwritten copies of H 73. By midsummer 1891, sheets 23–24 had found their way into packet 6, and sheet 73 into packet 14. The variorum has left them in these places, yet the manuscript evidence shows that they belong to packet 27. Packet 14 easily relinquishes H 73 since neither the paper nor the sewing holes nor the dating of the handwriting matches the other sheets there. The two sheets now in packet 6, however, do match the stationery and the handwriting period of the other sheets there, and in such a case the decisive factor must be the sewing holes. Those in packet 6 are slightly closer together than those in packet 27, and sheets 23–24 match the latter perfectly. With the removal of these sheets packet 6 is correctly assembled: H 25–27, 381. The correct assembly of packet 27 is shown in Table 8.

PACKET 27

Sheet	Poem	
H 144a	Good Morning—Midnight—	V425
b	I like to see it lap the Miles—	V585
c	It dont sound so terrible—quite—as it did—	V426
H 145a	I'll clutch—and clutch—	V427
b	Taking up the fair Ideal,	V428
c	The Moon is distant from the Sea—	V429
H 146a	It would never be Common—more—I said—	V430
b	Me—come! My dazzled face	V431
c	Do People moulder equally,	V432
H 147	Knows how to forget!	V433
H 148a	We talked as Girls do—	V586
b	Empty my Heart, of Thee—	V587
c	I cried at Pity—not at Pain—	V588
*H 23a	It's thoughts—and just One Heart—	V495
b	I know a place where Summer strives	V337
c	As far from pity, as complaint—	V496
*H 24a	I know that He exists.	V338
b	He strained my faith—	V497
c	I tend my flowers for thee—	V339
*H 73a	The Grass so little has to do,	V333
b	All the letters I can write	V334
c	I cannot dance upon my Toes—	V326

Table 8.—Proposed revision of packet 27. The sheets with an asterisk are transfers: H 23–24 from packet 6 and H 73 from packet 14.

Reordering Packets 10, 14, 23, and 26

One must agree with Mr. Johnson's handling of packets 23 and 26 and, in the main, of packets 10 and 14, the final group of Houghton packets to be discussed. Packet 10 currently has but one leaf, containing a single poem, though in 1891, according to Mrs. Todd's record book, several additional sheets were with it. Three of these sheets are now in packet 26 (H 47–49), and one is in packet 23 (H 46). The notebook further indicates that H 74, also now in packet 23, should go into packet 14. These moves, if effected, would arrange packets 10,

14 (plus H 70),* 23, and 26 as they stood in midsummer 1891 when Mrs. Todd cataloged the manuscripts and also, with the removal of H 172–74 from packet 26, as they were when the Houghton Library received them in 1950. After their arrival at the Houghton Library, however, Mr. Johnson examined the manuscript evidence afforded by paper, sewing holes, and handwriting and concluded that these packets were not in the original order in which Emily Dickinson had bound them. He then moved the errant sheets out of packets 10 and 14 (H 46–49, H 74) and back into packets 23 and 26 where they properly belong, in addition to correcting the placement of H 70 and returning H 172–74 to packet 26. I have examined each of these moves and agree that packets 23 and 26 now reflect their original order.

But this arrangement still leaves packet 10 with only one poem on one leaf—hardly enough to be termed a fascicle. I doubt that it was ever one of Emily Dickinson's fascicles. This sheet is actually a half sheet, separated at the fold from the other half, and contains the one poem "The feet of people walking home" (V7). It has been folded in thirds as though it had been intended for mailing to a friend rather than for binding into a fascicle. I suspect that it was lying loose among the poems that Lavinia found and that she, or Mrs. Todd, bound it with the four displaced sheets from packets 23 and 26. In midsummer 1891, then, Mrs. Todd assigned the number 10 to this false arrangement, and since the half sheet was on top, it received the blue penciled number. When Mr. Johnson returned the four displaced sheets to packets 23 and 26, where they belonged, this half sheet was left by itself. Since the number 10 on it seemed to indicate that it was rightly part of one of Emily Dickinson's fascicles, Mr. Johnson has let it remain at the Houghton Library as packet 10. It was probably not, however, part of one of Emily Dickinson's fascicles.

In spite of several changes, the problem of packet 14 is yet unresolved. Mr. Johnson transferred sheet 70 to packet 29 and

---

* For a discussion of the placement of H 70, see above, pp. 39–40.

sheet 74 to packet 23, and I have proposed shifting sheet 73 to packet 27. Even so, the packet remains a hodge-podge of sheets. With six of them remaining,[48] the packet has three different kinds of paper, two or three different periods of handwriting, and three sets of mismatched sewing holes.[49] The sheets are so unrelated that one might suspect they were parts of other gatherings. I have searched several times for the appropriate places in the other fascicles, and although possibilities appear, the manuscript evidence for any of them is not strong enough to establish proper places for these sheets. It is possible, of course, that these sheets might never have been bound by Emily Dickinson into her fascicles; the sewing holes might have come from the sheets having been bound with displaced sheets sometime between 1886 and 1891. Or perhaps some of the sheets may have constituted a small packet by themselves—H 75–77, for example. At any rate, the six sheets, so grouped, never formed one of Emily Dickinson's fascicles.

The History of the Houghton Packets

This discussion of the fascicles at the Houghton Library is summarized, and occasionally augmented, in Chart 1. The history of these manuscripts spans nearly a hundred years, and during this span there are five points at which the order of the manuscripts can be determined. In reverse chronology, they are the variorum arrangement (1952), the Houghton inventory (1950), Mrs. Todd's indexing (midsummer 1891), the Todd-Graves copying (1887–89), and Emily Dickinson's binding (1858–86). To trace the history of any one of Emily Dickinson's gatherings, one should read the chart from top to bottom; at the foot of each column is given the proposed reordering. For example, the first group has remained in its proper order all the while, and no reordering is necessary. The second group, however, was split into two by the time of the Todd-Graves copying, after which sheet 5 was shifted from one half to the other. In midsummer 1891 the halves were numbered as packets 2 and 3 and have remained divided ever since. They should be reunited.[50]

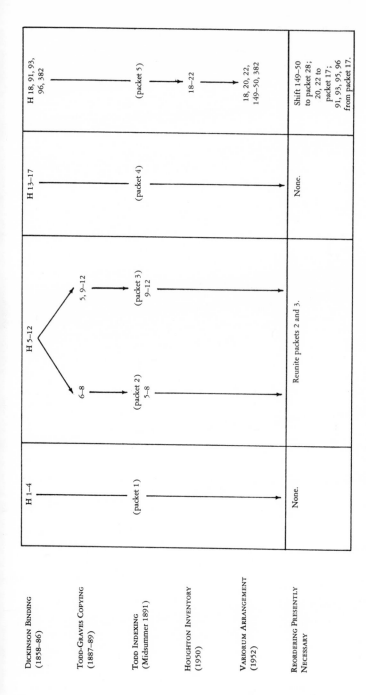

Chart 1.—History of the Fascicles now at the Houghton Library.

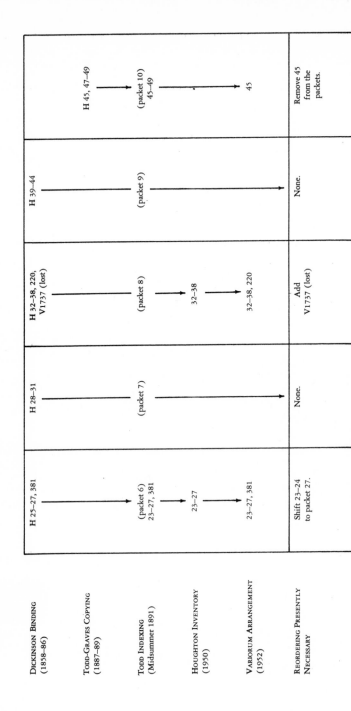

	DICKINSON BINDING (1858–66)	TODD-GRAVES COPYING (1887–89)	TODD INDEXING (Midsummer 1891)	HOUGHTON INVENTORY (1950)	VARIORUM ARRANGEMENT (1952)	REORDERING PRESENTLY NECESSARY
	H 25–27, 381	(packet 6) 23–27, 381	23–27	23–27, 381	Shift 23–24 to packet 27.
	H 28–31	(packet 7)			None.
	H 32–38, 220, V1737 (lost)	(packet 8)	32–38	32–38, 220	Add V1737 (lost)
	H 39–44	(packet 9)			None.
	H 45, 47–49	(packet 10) 45–49		45	Remove 45 from the packets.

Chart 1.—History of the Fascicles now at the Houghton Library (cont.).

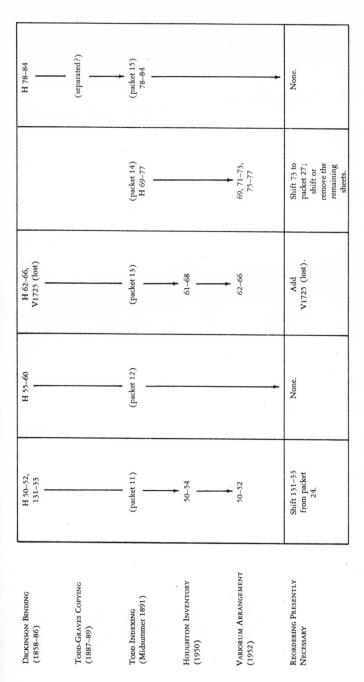

Chart 1.—History of the Fascicles now at the Houghton Library (cont.).

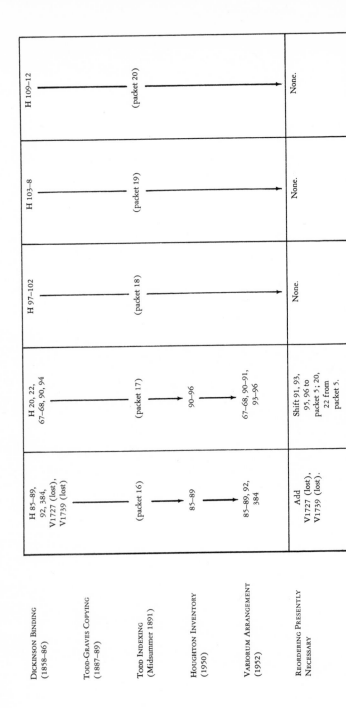

Chart 1.—History of the Fascicles now at the Houghton Library (cont.).

	DICKINSON BINDING (1858–86)	TODD-GRAVES COPYING (1887–89)	TODD INDEXING (Midsummer 1891)	HOUGHTON INVENTORY (1950)	VARIORUM ARRANGEMENT (1952)	REORDERING PRESENTLY NECESSARY
	H 85–89, 92, 384, V1727 (lost), V1739 (lost)	(packet 16)	85–89	85–89, 92, 384	Add V1727 (lost), V1739 (lost).
	H 20, 22, 67–68, 90, 94	(packet 17)	90–96	67–68, 90–91, 93–96	Shift 91, 93, 95, 96 to packet 5; 20, 22 from packet 5.
	H 97–102	(packet 18)			None.
	H 103–8	(packet 19)			None.
	H 109–12	(packet 20)			None.

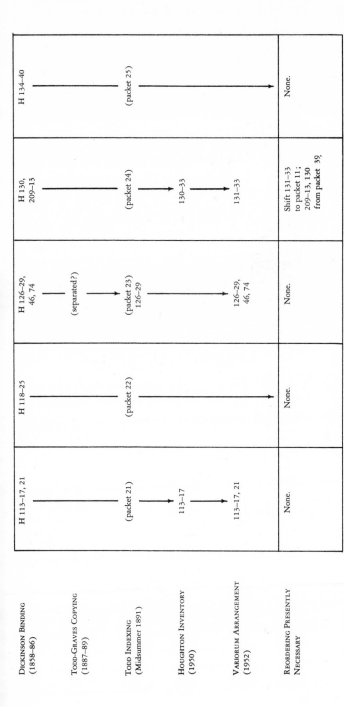

	H 113–17, 21	H 118–25	H 126–29, 46, 74	H 130, 209–13	H 134–40
Dickinson Binding (1858–86)					
Todd-Graves Copying (1887–89)	(packet 21)	(packet 22)	(separated?)	(packet 24)	(packet 25)
Todd Indexing (Midsummer 1891)	113–17		(packet 23) 126–29	130–33	
Houghton Inventory (1950)	113–17, 21		126–29, 46, 74	131–33	
Variorum Arrangement (1952)	None.	None.	None.	Shift 131–33 to packet 11; 209–13, 130 from packet 39;	None.
Reordering Presently Necessary					

Chart 1.—History of the Fascicles now at the Houghton Library (cont.).

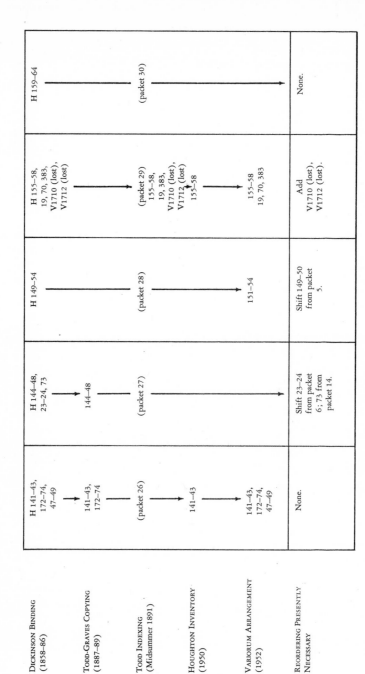

DICKINSON BINDING (1858–86)	H 141–43, 172–74, 47–49	H 144–48, 23–24, 73	H 149–54	H 155–58, 19, 70, 383, V1710 (lost), V1712 (lost)	H 159–64
TODD-GRAVES COPYING (1887–89)	141–43, 172–74	144–48			
TODD INDEXING (Midsummer 1891)	(packet 26)	(packet 27)	(packet 28)	(packet 29) 155–58, 19, 383, V1710 (lost), V1712 (lost) 155–58	(packet 30)
HOUGHTON INVENTORY (1950)	141–43			155–58 19, 70, 383	
VARIORUM ARRANGEMENT (1952)	141–43, 172–74, 47–49		151–54		
REORDERING PRESENTLY NECESSARY	None.	Shift 23–24 from packet 6; 73 from packet 14.	Shift 149–50 from packet 5.	Add V1710 (lost), V1712 (lost).	None.

Chart 1.—History of the Fascicles now at the Houghton Library (cont.).

DICKINSON BINDING (1858–86)	TODD-GRAVES COPYING (1887–89)	TODD INDEXING (Midsummer 1891)	HOUGHTON INVENTORY (1950)	VARIORUM ARRANGEMENT (1952)	REORDERING PRESENTLY NECESSARY
H 165–70		(packet 31) →→→→			None.
H 53–54, 61, 171		(packet 32) → 171–74 → 53–54, 61, 171			None.
? (not bound)	?	(packet 33) H 175–80 →→→→			None.
H 181–87		(packet 34) →→→→			None.
? (not bound)	?	(packet 35) H 188–93 →→→→			None.

Chart 1.—History of the Fascicles now at the Houghton Library (cont.).

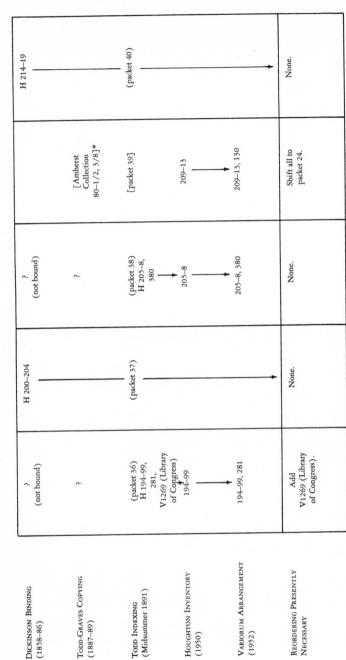

DICKINSON BINDING (1858–86)	? (not bound)	H 200–204	? (not bound)	[Amherst Collection 80–1/2, 3/8]*	H 214–19 →
TODD-GRAVES COPYING (1887–89)	?		?		
TODD INDEXING (Midsummer 1891)	(packet 36) H 194–99, 281, V1269 (Library of Congress) 194–99	(packet 37) →	(packet 38) H 205–8, 380 → 205–8	[packet 39]	(packet 40)
HOUGHTON INVENTORY (1950)	→ 194–99, 281		205–8	209–13 →	
VARIORUM ARRANGEMENT (1952)	194–99, 281		205–8, 380	209–13, 130	
REORDERING PRESENTLY NECESSARY	Add V1269 (Library of Congress).	None.	None.	Shift all to packet 24.	None.

* See the discussion of packet 80 in the text.

Chart 1.—History of the Fascicles now at the Houghton Library (cont.).

THE AMHERST COLLECTION

The Amherst Collection, in contrast to the collection at Harvard, does not pose many problems. Envelopes 96–110 contained only loose poems, generally on odds and ends of paper, and since their arrangement was an editorial one, Jay Leyda, who cataloged the Amherst Collection in 1957, removed these poems from the envelopes and arranged them alphabetically instead. Either order is purely arbitrary, and since the alphabetical arrangement is easier to work with than the old envelope order, it is preferable.

The fascicles at Amherst College do not present many problems either. Since those numbered 86–95 are unthreaded, we cannot be sure that the present grouping of sheets is the same as Emily Dickinson's. The farthest back that the order of these unbound fascicles can be traced is midsummer 1891, when Mrs. Todd cataloged them, and the notebook in which she entered the packet locations for unpublished poems shows that these ten packets are constituted now as then.[51]

Six packets at Amherst are bound (80–85), and consequently their history can be traced in full. Five of them (81–85) are without complications, since all evidence indicates that they are now ordered as Emily Dickinson bound them. Packet 80 is the lone exception.

Reconstructing Packet 80

As it now stands, packet 80 is incomplete. The variorum lists nineteen poems for it, and Mrs. Todd's 1891 notebook names the same nineteen, but when Emily Dickinson first bound the sheets together, the packet contained six additional poems. She assembled packet 80 as it is shown in Table 9. Asterisks mark the poems, now separated from the packet, that I am proposing be added to it. The additions come from two sources: (1) from certain scraps and (2) from poems whose manuscripts are now lost. It will be best to consider the scraps first.

Four of the poems to be added to packet 80 come from the three pieces of manuscript in the Amherst Collection that are reproduced in Figures 7, 8, 9, and 10. Mr. Leyda was the first

PACKET 80

Sheet	Poem	
80–1/2a	There is a word	V8
b	Through lane it lay—thro' bramble—	V9
(2) c	The Guest is gold and crimson—	V15
d	I counted till they danced so	V36
e	Before the ice is in the pools—	V37
f	By such and such an offering	V38
80–3/8a	It did not surprise me—	V39
b	When I count the seeds	V40
(8) c	*Bless God, he went as soldiers,	V147
d	*If I should cease to bring a Rose	V56
e	*One Sister have I in the house—	V14
80–9/4a	(conclusion of "One Sister")	(V14)
b	*"Lethe" in my flower,	V1730
c	*To venerate the simple days	V57
d	*I've got an arrow here.	V1729
(4) e	I robbed the Woods—	V41
f	A Day! Help! Help! Another Day!	V42
g	Could live—*did* live—	V43
h	If she had been the Mistletoe	V44
80–5/6a	My wheel is in the dark!	V10
b	There's something quieter than sleep	V45
(6) c	I keep my pledge.	V46
d	Heart! We will forget him!	V47
e	Once more, my now bewildered Dove	V48
f	Baffled for just a day or two—	V17
80–7	The face I carry with me—last—	V336

Table 9.—Proposed revision of packet 80. The poems marked with an asterisk are new additions. The numbers in parentheses along the left side indicate where the second leaf of a sheet begins.

to notice that the paper and handwriting of these pieces match packet 80, and when he cataloged the collection, he placed the three scraps in the folder for the packet, with the suggestion that they were "possibly from this fascicle."[52] A careful study shows that they do in fact belong here. The paper for packet 80 is lightly ruled stationery that has been folded in half by the manufacturer and embossed with a coat of arms through both leaves. The paper of these scraps is identical, and the placement

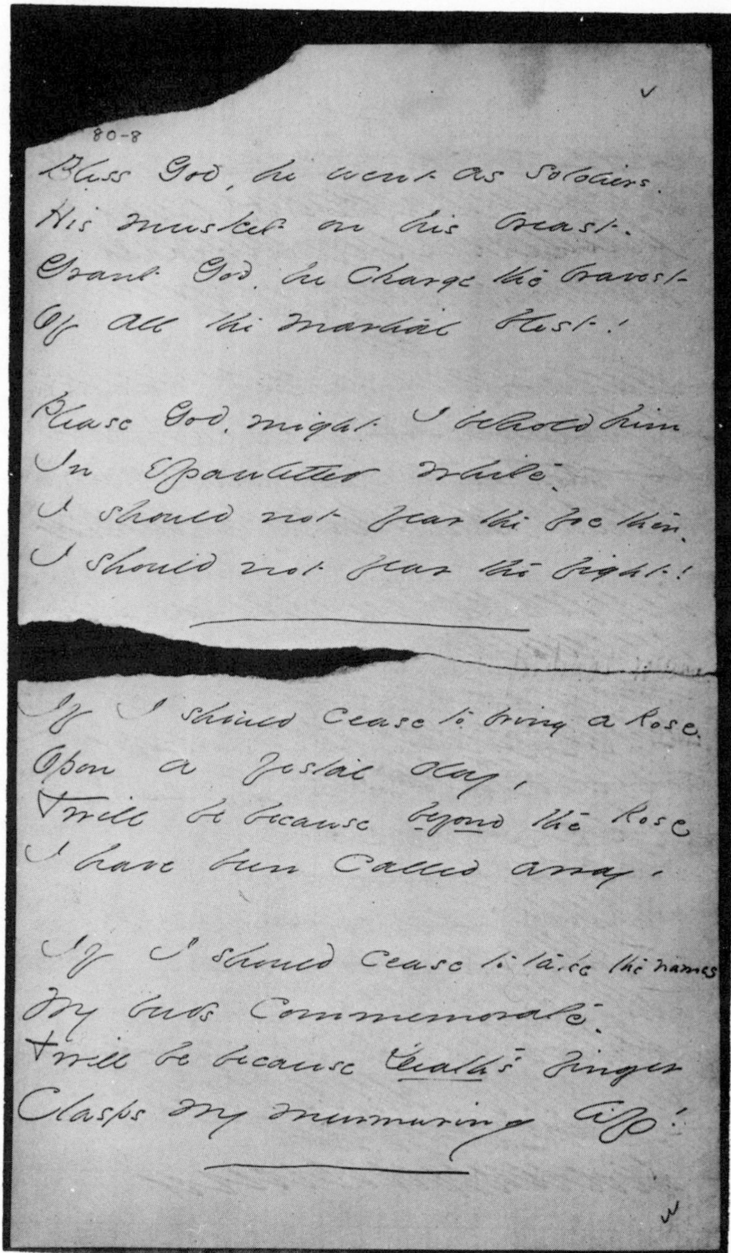

80-8

Bless God, he went as soldiers,
His musket on his breast—
Grant God, he charge the bravest
Of all the martial host—!

Please God, might I behold him
In epauletted white—
I should not fear the foe then—
I should not fear the fight!

If I should cease to bring a Rose
Upon a festal day,
Twill be because beyond the Rose
I have been called away—

If I should cease to take the names
My buds Commemorate—
Twill be because Death's finger
Clasps my murmuring lip!

Fig. 7.—Recto of leaf 80–8. By permission of the Amherst College Library.

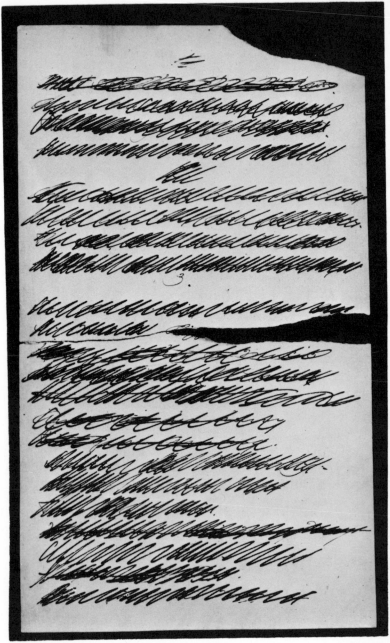

Fig. 8.—Verso of leaf 80–8. By permission of the Amherst College Library.

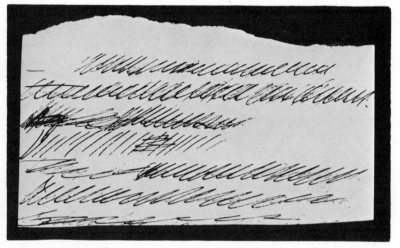

Fig. 9.—Recto of upper part of leaf 80–9. By permission of the Amherst College Library.

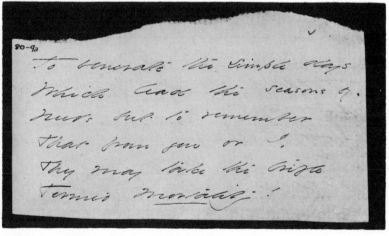

Fig. 10.—Verso of upper part of leaf 80–9. By permission of the Amherst College Library.

of the embossed design and its relation to the ruling establish that the two pieces in Figures 7 and 8 were the second leaf of sheet 80–3/8 and that the other piece in Figures 9 and 10 was the top part of the first leaf of sheet 80–9/4.* Confirmation that the three pieces do belong to packet 80 is the fact that Mrs. Todd marked an 80 on the transcripts for the three uncanceled poems on them.[53]

Altogether the three pieces contain four poems: one has been canceled heavily, one has a stanza missing, and only two are complete. The canceled sides of the three pieces can be deciphered without special equipment. They contain another version of "One Sister have I in our house" (V14), an effusive poem Emily wrote about Susan Dickinson, her sister-in-law, and sent across the hedge separating their houses.[54] The variorum does not include this canceled poem. This version has some special interest, however, for it shows that the poem was perhaps originally conceived in a different order than in the copy sent to Sue and that Emily Dickinson indicated the shift in stanzas by marking them 1, 2, 3, 5, 6, 4. She may have inadvertently copied the stanzas out of order, however, and then numbered them as a correction. The punctuation and capitaliza-

---

* Since the three pieces were not cataloged in their proper position, their numbers are out of sequence and, admittedly, are confusing. Mr. Leyda numbered leaves, not sheets as the Houghton Library had done; in proper order the five *sheets* for packet 80 are: 80–1/2, 80–3/8, 80–9/4, 80–5/6, and 80–7.

It should be noted that the stationery of 80–7 does not match the other sheets in packet 80 and that the date assigned to it by the variorum is four years later than the rest of the packet. This sheet has only one poem on it ("The face I carry with me—last" [V336]) and has been folded in thirds and addressed to someone whose name has been erased. Thus, binding the poem into packet 80 was clearly not Emily Dickinson's first intention for it. But the poem was there when Mrs. Todd indexed the manuscript in midsummer 1891, and it was there when she copied the packet in 1889. Since I am unable to prove or disprove that Emily Dickinson herself actually bound the poem into the packet, I have here left it where it has been since 1889 at least. But I note that the poem may not have been part of Emily Dickinson's grouping. Cf. the discussion of packet 10 above in this chapter.

tion are variant at times, and two words differ in this version:
"the" (line 1 here) reads "our" (line 1 in the copy to Sue),
and "And" (line 16 here) reads "Still" (line 20 in the copy
to Sue).[55] Parts of the canceled version are missing now, and
when such is the case, the reading of the copy sent to Sue is
here substituted in brackets:

1.

One Sister have I in the house—
And one a hedge away.
There's only one recorded—
But both belong to me.

2.

One came the road that I cam[e—]   5
And wore my last year's gown—
The other, as a bird her nest
Builded our hearts among.

3.

She did not sing as we did[—]
It was a [different tune—]   10
Herself to her a music
As Bumble bee of June.

5.

And still her hum
The years among,
Deceives the Butterfly;   15
And in her Eye
The Violets lie,
Mouldered this many May—

6.

I spilt the dew,
But took the morn—[56]
I chose this single star   20
From out the wide night's numbers—
Sue—forevermore!

4.

Today is far from childhood,
But up and down the hills,
I held her h[and the tighter—]   25
[Which shortened all the miles—]

The uncanceled side of the manuscript reproduced in Figures 9 and 10 originally formed the top section of the verso of 80–9.[57] At that time the single stanza on this piece of manuscript, beginning "To venerate the simple days," was not the only stanza to the poem. It was followed by another which, because of the mutilation of the manuscript, became separated from the first stanza and was subsequently lost. Fortunately, Mrs. Todd copied packet 80 before the mutilation occurred, and her transcript for the whole poem still survives to provide us with the complete text (Fig. 11).[58] When Mr. Johnson published this poem in the variorum, he limited it to the first stanza, though he noted that the text that had appeared in *Poems, Third Series* (1896) had had a second stanza. He then printed the second stanza separately in reduced type. In 1960, when he brought out a one-volume edition of Emily Dickinson's poetry, he omitted the variorum notes to the poems, and as a result, "To venerate the simple days" is there "standardized"—as claimed for that edition—with but one of its stanzas.[59]

Unlike "To venerate the simple days," the two uncanceled poems reproduced in Figure 7 are both complete, and Mr. Johnson published them in the variorum in full. But in the final line of "If I should cease to bring a Rose" (V56), the variorum reads "Claps" instead of "Clasps my murmuring lip!"[60] The variorum is also incorrect in the dating of these two poems. Emily Dickinson copied them, one after the other and probably only a few minutes apart, onto the same sheet of stationery in packet 80, yet the variorum has assigned the poems to two different years: the first (V147) to 1859 and the second (V56) to 1858. Since the rest of the poems on this sheet are dated 1858, one concludes that both of these should be too.

A piece of manuscript belonging to packet 80 is still missing. The second stanza of "To venerate the simple days" was on this piece along with two other poems whose holograph copies are now lost. Identifying these poems without the help of manuscript evidence might seem impossible, but Mrs. Todd, it will be remembered, at times marked the packet source of

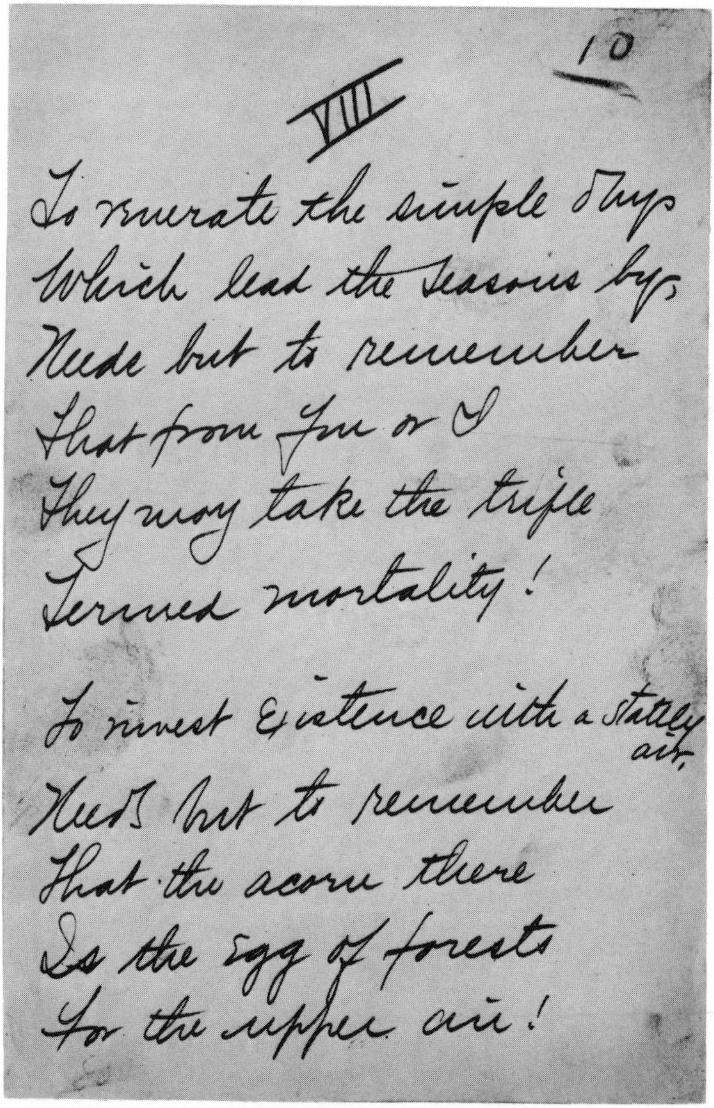
10

VIII

To venerate the simple days
Which lead the seasons by,
Needs but to remember
That from you or I
They may take the trifle
Termed mortality!

To invest existence with a stately air,
Needs but to remember
That the acorn there
Is the egg of forests
For the upper air!

Fig. 11.—Mabel Loomis Todd's transcript of "To venerate the simple days" (V57). By permission of the Amherst College Library.

poems on their transcripts. In the present instance she did so on transcripts for both of the missing poems from packet 80. The first is of " 'Lethe' in my flower" (V1730), on which Mrs. Todd's 80 is plainly visible.[61] The other transcript is of the poem "I've got an arrow here" (V1729). It was published in *Poems, Third Series* (1896), and during the course of the editing the 80 was erased from the transcript, but the number is still legible.[62] Mr. Johnson published both of these poems in the section of the variorum reserved for poems without manuscripts and without clue to their dating. These two can now be dated, since they were originally part of a sheet whose date is known. Assuming that the dating of the rest of the packet is correct, we can place these in the year 1858.

The Mutilation of Packet 80

The mutilation of packet 80 was not accidental, but quite deliberately done. The two leaves were cut out of the packet and the sewing holes trimmed off so that the leaves would not appear to have come from a packet. Then leaf 80–9 (Figs. 9 and 10) was carefully cut and leaf 80–8 (Figs. 7 and 8) was carefully torn, into two pieces each, so that the poems on the opposite sides of "One Sister have I in the house" would be left undamaged. Then the torn edge of 80–8 was torn again so that the two edges would not appear to match, and the top trim edge of both leaves was torn, apparently for no other reason than to make reassembly difficult. Finally, in black ink the sides containing "One Sister" were heavily canceled, with the line "Sue —forevermore!" canceled the heaviest of all.

The intent was obviously to destroy the effusive poem about Susan Dickinson. This could not be completely done without also destroying the poems on the opposite sides. The person responsible for the mutilation, however, did not want to destroy the other poems, and therefore the two leaves were carefully divided between the poems on the opposite sides so that they would be complete. But the mutilator erred in one place: he or she cut the poem "To venerate the simple days" in half, leaving its two stanzas on different pieces of paper. It is easy to see how it happened. Emily Dickinson frequently drew a line below a poem to indicate its end. The last line of the first stanza of "To venerate" has an italicized word—there is a short line drawn beneath the word *mortality* (Fig. 10)—and since that italicized word comes near the center of the page, the line beneath it appears, at first glance, to be Emily Dickinson's signal that the poem is finished.

Such a mistake in reading the manuscripts is unlikely to have been Emily Dickinson's. She may have had cause to feel antagonism toward her sister-in-law, but we may be sure that it was not she who sought to destroy her own poem. We may be sure, for there is evidence that the sheets were still intact when Mrs. Todd first handled them: her transcript of the now incomplete poem ("To venerate") is itself complete (Fig. 11). But even more conclusive is the fact that Mrs. Todd wrote at the head of the poem "If I should cease to bring a Rose" the following note to herself: "[?] for final volume." Her writing, now erased but mostly legible, falls on both sides of the tear in this leaf (see Fig. 12), indicating that Mrs. Todd received the packet in its original condition and that it was mutilated thereafter.

The notebook in which Mrs. Todd listed the packet poems yet unpublished in midsummer 1891 does not list the poems on the fragments belonging to packet 80 even though they were yet unpublished. Thus the mutilation occurred sometime after Mrs. Todd first received the packet but before she did the indexing in 1891. She had a dislike for Susan Dickinson,[63] but it is unlikely that she was the mutilator of the manuscript. Like Emily Dickinson, she had an intimate acquaintance with the manuscripts and would not have mistaken the two stanzas of "To venerate the simple days" for separate poems, especially since she had already copied the poem in full. The mutilator did not want the poem "One Sister have I in the house" to be published and therefore not only canceled the poem, but disfigured the manuscript pieces so that an editor could not put them together

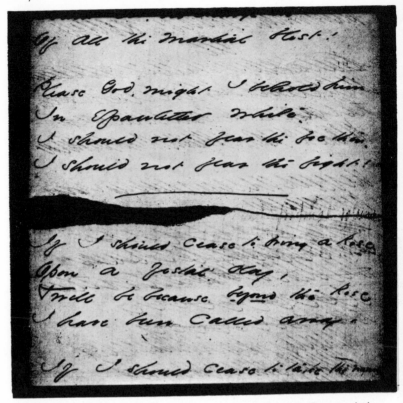

Fig. 12.—Mabel Loomis Todd's note on leaf 80–8. By permission of the Amherst College Library; photograph courtesy of the Wisconsin State Crime Laboratory.

again. Mrs. Todd would have had no cause to do so since she was herself that editor. Besides, such an action goes directly against the grain of her respectful handling of the manuscripts.

The only other people with ready access to the manuscripts between 1887 and 1891 were Emily Dickinson's sister and brother, Lavinia and Austin. One of them, or both, was responsible for the defacement of packet 80. All the Dickinsons had viewed Austin's marriage to Susan Huntington Gilbert with especial favor, but disappointment came early. Austin was destined to bear a burden of domestic troubles, and his sisters, just a hedge away, also suffered under the influence of their sister-in-law.[64] When Mrs. Todd edited Emily Dickinson's letters in 1894, she found that

> although in general both Lavinia and Austin approved of whatever I did or did not do in the way of editing, leaving decision as to what to print and what to leave out entirely to me, they did make one request, namely, that I omit certain passages, references to a relative then living, in some of the early letters.[65]

The relative was Austin's wife, Sue. To insure that her name would not be printed, Austin went through the letters deleting it and passages about her. He erased when the letters were in pencil; when they were in ink, he used heavy cancelation, substituted readings, and even cut out undesirable paragraphs with scissors.[66] The poem "One Sister have I in the house" would have gained neither Lavinia's nor Austin's approval for publication, and its fate is sufficiently similar to the offending passages in Emily Dickinson's letters that the responsibility for its defacement must rest with her kin.

The History of Packet 80

In brief, the history of packet 80 is this. When Mrs. Todd received the manuscripts from Lavinia, the sheets belonging to this packet were still whole, but had become separated into two groups. Two sheets, 80–1/2 and 80–3/8, were considered to be a packet by themselves and were transcribed on the World machine while the other sheets were copied by Mrs. Todd by hand (Table 10). The first group she came to regard as packet 39 and the second as packet 80. Since the poem "One Sister have I in the house" covered parts of two different sheets (see Table 9), their separation left part of the poem in what Mrs. Todd thought was packet 39 and part in packet 80. Mrs. Todd discovered that the two parts belonged together and that, therefore, the two groups of sheets really formed only one of Emily Dickinson's fascicles. She then reunited the sheets, thereby eliminating packet 39 entirely. She had already placed a 39 on

PACKET 80

Sheet	Poem	Surviving Transcripts
80–1/2a	V8	World (purple) on paper P
b	V9	World (purple) on paper P
c	V15	World (purple) on paper P
d	V36	World (purple) on paper P
e	V37	World (purple) on paper P
f	V38	World (purple) on paper P
80–3/8a	V39	World (purple) on paper P
b	V40	World (purple) on paper P
c	V147	World (purple) on paper P
d	V56	World (purple) on paper P
e	V14	. . . . . .
80–9/4a	(conclusion to V14)	
b	V1730	Mabel Loomis Todd on paper Q
c	V57	Mabel Loomis Todd on paper Q
d	V1729	Mabel Loomis Todd on paper Q
e	V41	. . . .
f	V42	Mabel Loomis Todd on paper Q
g	V43	Mabel Loomis Todd on paper Q
h	V44	Mabel Loomis Todd on paper Q
80–5/6a	V10	Mabel Loomis Todd on paper Q
b	V45	Mabel Loomis Todd on paper Q
c	V46	Mabel Loomis Todd on paper Q
d	V47	Mabel Loomis Todd on paper Q
e	V48	Mabel Loomis Todd on paper Q
f	V17	Mabel Loomis Todd on paper Q
80–7	V336	Mabel Loomis Todd on paper Q

Table 10.—Transcript pattern for packet 80.

several of the transcripts, and these numbers were now changed to 80.[67] Shortly thereafter, Austin and/or Lavinia found the effusive poem about Sue and proceeded to deface the manuscripts as described above. The mutilated fragments so closely resembled the other odds and ends of paper upon which Emily Dickinson wrote poems that Mrs. Todd transferred them to an envelope among the scraps. The location guides were again changed, this time from 80 to "scrap."[68] In 1955 the variorum editor suggested that two of the three fragments resembled verses copied into packets.[69] In 1957 when Jay Leyda cataloged the Amherst Collection, he associated all three fragments with packet 80, suggesting that they were "possibly from this fascicle." They, as well as the fragment still missing, do in fact belong to it.

PUBLICATION AND RECEPTION
OF THE SECOND SERIES

When the galley proof of *Poems, Second Series* began arriving in mid-August 1891, Mrs. Todd had already finished the indexing of the manuscripts. She allotted the remainder of the month to reading the galleys and to comparing each poem on them with Emily Dickinson's holograph copy. The Todds were planning a short vacation before the fall term commenced, and Mrs. Todd hoped to finish checking the proof before she left. It was slow in coming, however, and when she left on September 2 for a two-week trip to Wyoming, New York, the task was only half completed. So determined was Mrs. Todd that the poems should be published properly that she directed the remaining proof be sent to her in New York and took the original manuscripts with her in order to check the poems. Still the proof was slow, and she returned to Amherst with the galleys done but with the plate proofs yet to come. These revealed further errors, and even though the printers had the book on the press, Thomas Niles ordered them to lift it and to await Mrs. Todd's final corrections. On October 6 she could at last write to Colonel Higginson, "I believe there are *no* errors now, and I hope the book can proceed to see the light soon."[70] The printers were very busy, however, and another month elapsed before *Poems, Second Series* appeared on November 9, 1891.

The publication of this volume ended the first phase in the nineteenth-century editing of Emily Dickinson's poetry, 1886–91. Thereafter Colonel Higginson would no longer be available as a coeditor, and Mrs. Todd would assume full responsibility. Her copying of poems, except for occasional scraps, was over, for she and Miss Graves had copied all the fascicles, providing her with nearly a thousand transcripts that she could use in coming series. These transcripts she had classified according to poetic merit and had listed in the leather-covered notebook. Mrs. Todd had anticipated that there would be at least ten volumes of Emily Dickinson's poetry, and the 1891 notebook was to be her guide in selecting the contents.

Meanwhile, the reviewers cast the same bewildered glances at the second series as they had at the first. Again they raised a critical fuss over Emily Dickinson's form, or lack of it, at the same time that they admired the poet's penetrating perception and the breadth of her understanding. "Miss Dickinson," one of them wrote, "was evidently born to be the despair of reviewers."[71] Their published bewilderment, however, did not seem to affect the reading public. The volume sold nearly as well as the earlier one had, and the editors began receiving letters requesting that the remaining poems be released to the public. One reviewer with foresight predicted: ". . . the world will not rest satisfied till every scrap of her writings, letters as well as literature, has been published."[72] The first phase in the early editing of Emily Dickinson's poetry concluded with great promise, it seemed, for the future.

CHAPTER III

1891–1896: The Third Series in the Variorum

The second phase in the nineteenth-century editing (1891–96) had actually begun before the first ended. According to *Ancestors' Brocades,* Mrs. Todd made a preliminary selection of poems for a third series on July 16, 1891.[1] At this time Mrs. Todd was just beginning the indexing of the manuscripts and was still awaiting the proof of *Poems, Second Series.* Her faith in the poems was so firm that while the second series was yet unpublished and the public response unknown, she was at work selecting pieces for yet another volume. She again turned to the store of transcripts in her possession, and as she went through them choosing those she thought should be included, she wrote the words "3rd Series" on the transcripts she selected.[2] But the work of completing the notebook listing and of seeing the second series through the press engaged Mrs. Todd's efforts so thoroughly that a third series was temporarily forgotten. Meanwhile, Mrs. Todd's interest in Emily Dickinson's letters had increased, and instead of turning to a new volume of poetry after the second series was published, she began collecting and copying the letters that could be located.

Interest in the poetry, however, was never far from Mrs. Todd's mind, nor from Lavinia's. In the midst of collecting letters, Mrs. Todd, at Lavinia's request, suggested to Thomas Niles that instead of publishing a full edition of poems like the first two series, the firm would do well to bring out an Emily Dickinson yearbook in which a short epigrammatic quotation would be provided for each day of the year.[3] Niles expressed interest, and Mrs. Todd turned once more to her store of transcripts, this time writing "Yearbook" on the ones containing suitable quotations.[4] She was enthusiastic, for this venture gave her an opportunity to use the poems she had classified C. Too flawed to be published in full, these poems nevertheless contained occasional bolts of melody that would serve very well as material for a yearbook. By May 21, 1892, she had "200 selections for it already,"[5] but the volume was not to appear: Lavinia had changed her mind again. Instead of a yearbook, she now pressed Mrs. Todd to finish the letters, so the idea was abandoned for the moment.[6]

More than two and a half years later, Mrs. Todd published the *Letters of Emily Dickinson* in two volumes. The task of editing them had required nearly three full years of work. The poems had been immediately available, but the letters had to be gathered, some from reluctant hands, in order to be published. The task was often delicate, for New England tradition ruled that personal letters were a private trust never to be made public. Trying to locate letters and then trying to gain permission to use them took Mrs. Todd all the way to Colorado Springs, and frequently even after copies had been gained, parts had to be omitted in deference to the personal wishes of the recipients. The process was much too slow for Lavinia. She could not understand why the letters should be dated or arranged in an order, and in her impatience she became edgy. Finally, after three years of emotional strain and editorial difficulties, the two volumes appeared on November 21, 1894, saving a good many letters that undoubtedly would otherwise have been destroyed and a good many that in fact were.[7]

Little had actually been done about the poems during the years Mrs. Todd worked on the letters. Though she had twice turned to her store of transcripts and had written "3rd Series" and "Yearbook" on some of them, both projects had been abandoned before they really got under way. Some poems had appeared in magazines, and more had been included in *Letters* (1894).[8] But the reading public, who knew that more manuscripts existed and who, as one reviewer predicted, would "not rest satisfied" until all were published, had waited in vain for more than three years for a new volume of poems. With the *Letters* barely off her hands, Mrs. Todd wrote to E. D. Hardy, the successor to Niles as head of Roberts Brothers, that she had "unpublished poems enough for at least six more volumes like the first Series and Second." "Sometime we may want them," she continued, "but in the meantime how does the idea of an 'Emily Dickinson Year Book' strike you?"[9] Mrs. Todd herself was again enthusiastic, predicting that it would be "the most brilliant year-book ever issued."[10] Mr. Hardy was more cautious, requesting that a decision be deferred until the first of the following year, 1895, in order to see how well the *Letters* sold.[11] They apparently did not sell well enough to suit Hardy, for the yearbook project was abandoned permanently.

The rejection of a yearbook, however, did not mean that a new series of poems was immediately agreed upon. Most of 1895 elapsed before Mrs. Todd approached Colonel Higginson about editing a new volume. She visited him at his home in Cambridge on September 24, 1895. Then 71, he had been ill for some time and could offer her no assistance. Lavinia of course wanted more poems published, and since Roberts Brothers had by then agreed to a new volume, Mrs. Todd edited the third series by herself.[12]

Although poor health forbade his being coeditor, Colonel Higginson did have a part, both direct and indirect, in the editing of the third series. A few of the poems in it had also been included in the preliminary selections of the first two series, only to be cut out before publication, and the transcripts for these poems bear editorial markings that Higginson had made when preparing the poems for press in 1890 or in 1891. For example, the changes in punctuation and capitalization on the 1896 printer's copy of "I live with Him—I see His face" (see Fig. 1) were Colonel Higginson's. The Latin title to this poem, *Numen Lumen*, also was his, as were four of the English titles in the 1896 volume: *Alpine Glow* ("Our lives are Swiss"), *Wedded* ("A solemn thing—it was—I said"), *Unwarned* (" 'Tis Sunrise—Little Maid—Hast Thou"), and *Farewell* ("Tie the Strings to my Life, My Lord").[13] He was responsible, too, for some of the textual alterations in the third series. He was probably the one who marked out the final two stanzas of "A solemn thing —it was—I said" so that they were not printed,[14] and in the interest of rhyme he altered the wording of line 8 of " 'Tis Sunrise—Little Maid—Hast Thou."[15]

Viewed from another angle, Higginson's part in editing the third series was quite indirect. Mrs. Todd had the sole responsibility for the volume, and the editorial suggestions that Higginson had made on the transcripts four or five years earlier had to gain her approval now in order to reach print. That she not only retained all the titles he had suggested—including one Latin title, which she had always disliked—but also added a great many of her own testifies to the strength of his indirect influence. Even without his serving as coeditor, the third series was on the whole a close relative to the first two. The public had so enthusiastically welcomed the first and second series that Mrs. Todd continued the same editorial practice when she edited the new one. She punctuated poems, altered them, and in spite of an aversion to titles, titled many of them. In fact, the 1896 volume has more titles and more textual deviations than the previous selections had had. When faced with editing a volume of the poems alone, Mrs. Todd did not renounce the editorial practice that she and Colonel Higginson had effected. She appears to have extended it.[16]

The extension was not, I believe, entirely deliberate. In addition to the third series, Mrs. Todd was putting her own book *Stars and Telescopes* through the press as well as three others: her father's history of an expedition to Africa, an astronomy book by her husband, and *A Cycle of Sonnets* written by an anonymous friend.[17] Her time for doing this work was limited, for she and David Todd were sailing in the early spring for Japan, where once again her husband was conducting an expedition to observe a total solar eclipse. At first Mrs. Todd suggested to Mr. Hardy that the proof for the third series be sent to her in Japan,[18] but Hardy apparently wanted her to complete everything before her departure. With little time for steady judgment and for checking the proof of each poem against the original manuscript as she had carefully done with the first two series, Mrs. Todd pushed the volume to completion. In doing so, several printer's errors went uncorrected, as did a surprisingly large number of her own misreadings of the manuscripts.[19] The result is that the third series appears to be the most altered of the three nineteenth-century editions. It was probably not deliberately so.

With all the proof returned to Roberts Brothers but with the volume yet unpublished, Mrs. Todd left for Japan in April. *Poems, Third Series* was issued on September 1, 1896, while she was still away.[20]

THE 1896 PRINTER'S COPY

Poems, Third Series is unique among the nineteenth-century editions in that its printer's copy is the only one to survive.[21] The 1896 printer's copy is of special interest because by comparing it with Emily Dickinson's originals, with other transcripts, and with the printed versions, the full textual history of these poems can be determined. The printer's copy is thus an important document that can greatly aid an editor. The variorum editor at times did not use it effectively.

The variorum notes, for example, say that the text of "Not any higher stands the Grave" (V1256) followed the fair copy that Emily Dickinson had sent to Colonel Higginson (BPL Higg 38), not the semifinal draft in packet 93. A comparison of the printer's copy for this poem[22] with the transcript pattern for packet 93, however, indicates that the reverse is true. Packet 93 was in Mrs. Todd's possession, and the transcript from which this poem was published matches the most common paper Mrs. Todd used for copying it. In transcribing the poem from the semifinal draft in packet 93, Mrs. Todd chose the same two alternate readings that Emily Dickinson herself had chosen when she sent the copy to Higginson; thus since the two texts are the same, the third series printing appears to derive from the fair copy sent to Higginson, though it in fact did not.

The variorum lists one surviving manuscript for the poem "Few, yet enough" (V1596). Emily Dickinson sent this manuscript across the hedge to Sue, her sister-in-law, and signed it "Emily." The variorum does not note that another manuscript must have existed. Mrs. Todd published the poem in the third series,[23] and she must have had another manuscript source, since, because of the animosity between her and Susan Dickinson, she did not have access to the manuscripts in Sue's possession. Another poem published in the third series, "Father—I bring thee—not Myself" (V217), has a variant version beginning "Savior! I've no one else to tell." Mr. Johnson believes that the variant copy was sent to Sue, since there is a penciled note in the upper right margin of the manuscript: "S.H.D.'s copy—". The manuscript, however, was most likely not sent to Sue, for Mrs. Todd made a transcript of it,[24] and she did not have the opportunity to copy Sue's poems. The variant version, unlike other poems Emily Dickinson sent, has never been folded and is neither signed nor addressed.[25] The penciled note was not Sue's (the handwriting is quite unlike hers), but Martha Dickinson Bianchi's—made after Mrs. Todd copied the manuscript and returned it to Lavinia.[26]

Since the holograph copy for "My life closed twice before its close" (V1732) is now lost, the printer's copy for this well-known poem (Fig. 13) must supply our text.[27] An editor, however, should not accept this text without question,[28] for the printer's copy is not fully trustworthy in two regards. The spelling of "befel" in line 6 may not be Emily Dickinson's. The poet, it is true, spelled many words according to her own lights, but this would be the only instance of "befel," while she is known to have spelled "befall," "befallen," and "befalling" with

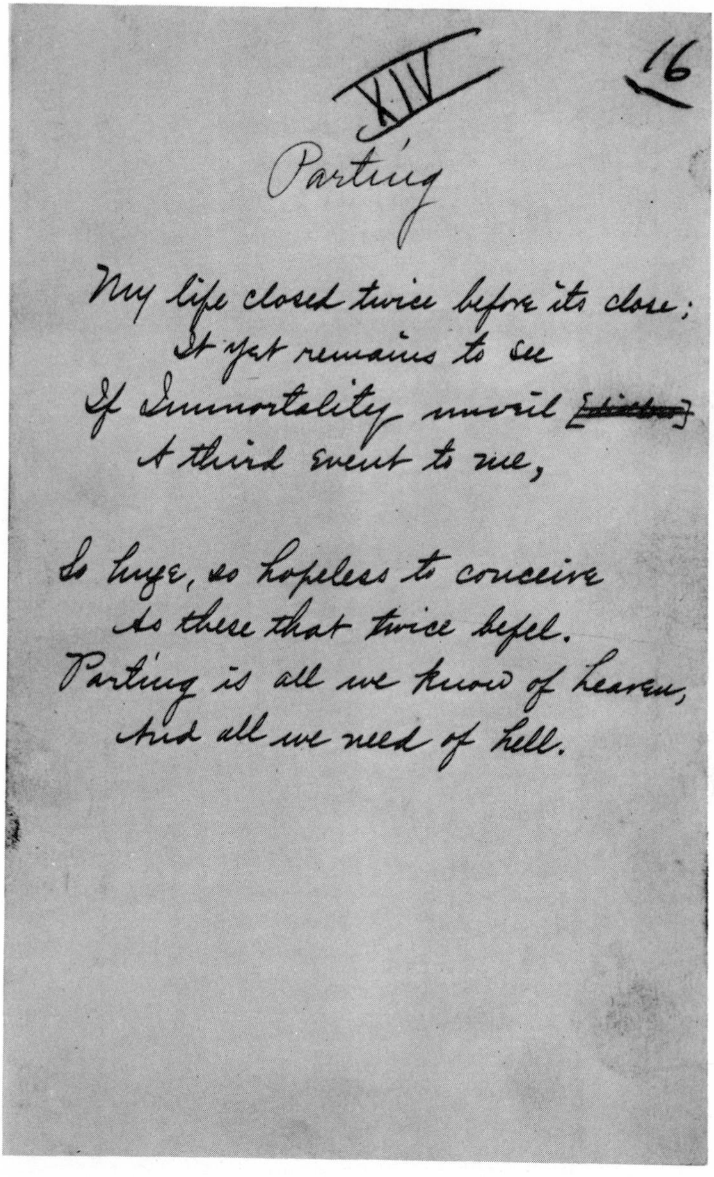

Parting

My life closed twice before its close;
 It yet remains to see
If Immortality unveil ~~a third~~
 A third event to me,

So huge, so hopeless to conceive
 As these that twice befel.
Parting is all we know of heaven,
 And all we need of hell.

Fig. 13.—1896 printer's copy of V1732. By permission of the Amherst College Library.

double *l*'s.[29] Moreover, Mrs. Todd usually regularized Emily
Dickinson's spellings before sending them to press. "Befel" may
be her own preference, for she not only sent the printer's copy
to Roberts Brothers with this spelling unchanged, but when she
made another transcript for *Scribner's Magazine,* it had the same
spelling.[30] The second reading on the 1896 printer's copy that
is not to be trusted is the alternate "disclose" (see Fig. 13).
Although the word may seem characteristic of Emily Dickinson's
wordplay ("My life *closed* twice before its *close*"), I suggest
that it was Mrs. Todd's. It is similar to other changes Mrs. Todd
made in the poems, such as the alteration of the fourth line of
"These are the days when Birds come back" (V130) in which
she destroyed a near rhyme in order to capture a *double en-
tendre.*[31] Furthermore, the appearance of "disclose" on the transcript is unlike any of Emily Dickinson's own alternates. When
Mrs. Todd entered these on a transcript, she either placed them
one over the other within brackets or she marked the appropriate
word in the text and entered the other suggestion at the foot of
the page (see Figs. 14–20). In all of the hundreds of surviving
transcripts there is no other example of her placing Emily Dickinson's suggestion to the side of the line and enclosing it in
square brackets. "Disclose" is probably Mrs. Todd's own word
enclosed in square brackets and placed to the side to keep it
separated from the regular text but close enough to serve as a
possible future alteration.[32]

Copies and Recopies

The printer's copy of " 'Twas just this time, last year, I
died" (V445) is also unreliable.[33] The manuscript for the poem
survives in packet 32, and the variorum lists the final two
stanzas as having been altered when published in the third
series. The final two stanzas, however, appear on the transcript
exactly as they do in the published version. Was there, then, a
variant holograph from which the printer's copy was made? The
answer is No. The printer's copy consists of two different sheets
of paper, the first of which exactly matches the rest of the paper
used in copying packet 32 and has an accurate copy of the text

of that packet; the second sheet, the one containing the variant stanzas, does not match its mate and the rest of the paper used for copying packet 32. Mrs. Todd, no doubt, originally copied the poem accurately onto two sheets of matching paper. At some later time she recopied the second sheet incorporating alterations into the final two stanzas. To the unwary it might appear that the transcript is trustworthy, but the transcript pattern shows it to be merely a "recopy" with alterations.

The difference between a first copy and a recopy is the difference between reliable and unreliable. Mrs. Todd tried to be faithful to the manuscripts in copying them; as Millicent Todd Bingham has said: "My mother was scrupulous about this. Any changes from the original text, whether of spelling or wording, were made subsequently on her own manuscripts [transcripts] and are plainly indicated."[34] Mrs. Todd's copies, then, apart from errors in transcribing, are important sources for poems and variants of poems now lost. In making a second or later copy of a poem, Mrs. Todd was not so exact, and these recopies contain readings that were not Emily Dickinson's.

An editor needs to observe this distinction carefully. The publishing history of "I measure every Grief I meet" (V561) illustrates the danger of being unwary. Miss Graves made the transcript of the poem; when Mrs. Todd prepared it for press, she altered lines 12 and 16 in pencil and crossed out stanza 4. She also introduced alterations into stanzas 5, 6, 7, and 10, but these stanzas she recopied, inserting them among the others in Miss Graves' handwriting.[35] In 1947 Millicent Todd Bingham contributed an article to the *New England Quarterly* in which she sought to publish a corrected version.[36] Since Emily Dickinson's holograph was not available to her, she published the poem from the transcript in the 1896 printer's copy, taking Mrs. Todd's recopying at face value and assuming one of her alterations (line 16) to be a correction of an error by Miss Graves. The result was a text in which the missing stanza was at last restored, but which was marred by a continuation of the alterations in stanzas 5, 6, 7, and 10 and by the introduction of yet another in line 16.

If one understands the distinction between a copy and a recopy, the transcript for "I measure every Grief I meet" is not difficult to evaluate properly, since the variety of handwriting and paper gives it away. A more difficult instance, but fortunately one that has tripped no one, is the transcript for "It will be Summer—eventually" (V342).[37] When published in the third series, the poem had been considerably altered. All of the changes were plainly indicated on the printer's copy of the poem with the exception of those in the third and fourth stanzas; here the changes were not indicated on the transcript but had been incorporated into the text in recopying. Since the paper is one Mrs. Todd frequently used in copying packet poems, the transcript appears to be a first, and therefore accurate, copy. Although the nature of the variants raises suspicion that they are editorial emendations (they produce a rhyme where the extant manuscript has none), the transcript could not be entirely discounted until the first copy itself was found. This was located among the transcripts in the Amherst Collection, and on it Eben Jenks Loomis, Mrs. Todd's father and himself a minor poet, had suggested alterations for the third and fourth stanzas which Mrs. Todd had included when she recopied the poem.[38]

Unlike the recopies just discussed, the variant transcript of the poem "Of Tolling Bell I ask the cause" (V947) is probably a reliable copy of a lost manuscript.[39] When the poem was published in the third series, it differed considerably from the manuscript version in packet 91. The packet version reads:

> Of Tolling Bell I ask the cause?
> "A Soul has gone to Heaven"
> I'm answered in a lonesome tone—
> Is Heaven then a Prison?
>
> That Bells should ring till all should know   5
> A Soul had gone to Heaven
> Would seem to me the more the way
> A Good News should be given.

> 5. know] hear

The text in the third series (p. 181) reads:

> If tolling bell I ask the cause.
>   'A soul has gone to God,'
> I'm answered in a lonesome tone;
>   Is heaven then so sad?
>
> That bells should joyful ring to tell   5
>   A soul had gone to heaven,
> Would seem to me the proper way
>   A good news should be given.

The variorum editor judged all the differences between these two texts to be editorial alterations. Many of them in fact are, but the transcript that served as printer's copy in 1896 (Fig. 14) has variant readings that are probably authentic. The paper used for this transcript is not a common one; however, each of the five other poems copied onto the surviving examples has an accurate text.[40] Packet 91, which contains the only surviving manuscript for "Of Tolling Bell I ask the cause," has a consistent transcript pattern that does not include this paper. Thus it would seem that the printer's copy of the poem is an accurate copy of an authentic variant, now lost, that was not part of packet 91.

Admittedly, Mrs. Todd's marking "(original)" after the second alternate at the foot of the sheet is strange. It could mean that Emily Dickinson's reading for line 7 was "more the way" and that the reading in line 7 itself was Mrs. Todd's emendation. It is probable, however, that the marking simply means that the starred words in the text and the alternate reading below were originally in reversed positions in the manuscript from which Mrs. Todd copied the poem. Neither this alternate nor the first alternate appears in the packet text, printed above, and the first alternate is not marked strangely—all of which suggests that another manuscript supplied the text for the transcript. The packet text itself has only one alternate ("hear"), and this Mrs. Todd later entered, in pencil, above the corresponding word in line 5 of the transcript. One concludes, therefore, that Mrs. Todd made the transcript used as the printer's copy from another holograph version, a variant which is now lost, and that she

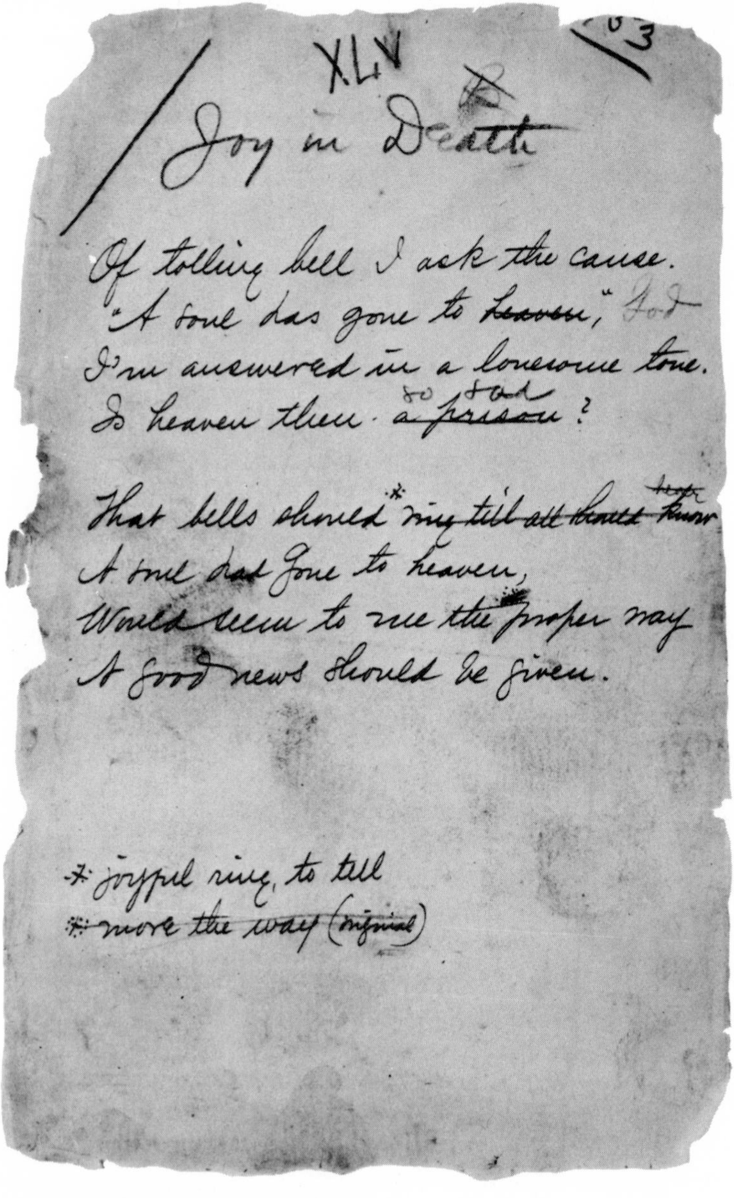

XLIV

Joy in Death

Of tolling bell I ask the cause.
"A soul has gone to heaven," God
I'm answered in a lonesome tone.
Is heaven then a prison? so sad

That bells should ring to tell all should know
A soul has gone to heaven,
Would seem to me the proper way
A good news should be given.

* joyful ring, to tell
* more the way (original)

Fig. 14.—1896 printer's copy of V947. By permission of the Amherst College Library.

added the alternate "hear" to the transcript upon comparing the two versions. With the readings for line 7 reversed, the transcript in the printer's copy probably represents one of Emily Dickinson's own variant manuscripts.[41]

Texts for Lost Manuscripts

During the years since 1896 the holographs for several of the poems in the third series have become lost. The printer's copy, divested of all editing, should become our source for the texts since, except in the case of recopies, it is the source closest to Emily Dickinson's own manuscripts. Twice the variorum editor did not examine the printer's copy for such poems, and each time the text that he prints is inadequate.

There is now, for example, but one manuscript for the poem "Who has not found the Heaven—below" (V1544). In it the final two lines appear:

> For Angels rent the House next our's,
> Wherever we remove—

Mr. Johnson, upon comparing these lines with the text in the third series, concluded that "the source of the published text, not located, was a variant copy, for the two final lines read:

> God's residence is next to mine,
> His furniture is love."[42]

The variorum editor did not pursue the matter further. If he had examined the 1896 printer's copy for the poem (Fig. 15), he would have learned that the published version derived from a semifinal draft, and his account of the poem in the variorum would not have omitted the alternate "livery."[43]

No autograph copy is known for the poem "Sweet hours have perished here" (V1767). The variorum notes to the poem say that "it was first published in *CP* (1924) [*Complete Poems* (1924)], 235, and is here reproduced from that text."[44] The note is erroneous, however, for the poem was first published in 1896 in *Poems, Third Series* (p. 163). Since Mrs. Bianchi did not have a manuscript of the poem, her text in *Complete Poems*

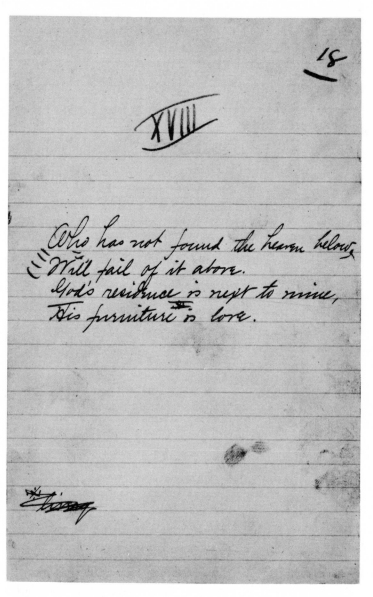

XVIII

Who has not found the heaven below
Will fail of it above.
God's residence is next to mine,
His furniture is love.

Fig. 15.—1896 printer's copy of V1544. By permission of the Amherst College Library.

(1924) came directly from the one in the third series, reproducing it exactly. Unfortunately, Mrs. Todd had altered line 2 of the printer's copy while preparing the poem for press (Fig. 16).[45] Since Mr. Johnson took his text from Mrs. Bianchi and Mrs. Bianchi took hers from the third series, Mrs. Todd's unauthorized emendation has been retained in all subsequent appearances of the poem, including the variorum and *Complete Poems* (1960).[46] From the 1896 printer's copy we also learn that the poem came from a semifinal draft and that "shadows" in the fourth line of the published text was Emily Dickinson's alternate for the word "fallow."[47]

The variorum did use the printer's copy as text for some eighteen poems whose holographs were not found. Mr. Johnson's policy was to reproduce Mrs. Todd's transcripts as they were first copied, before the editorial pencil was applied. His reproductions, however, are not always consistent or accurate regarding stanza arrangement, punctuation, and textual readings. For example, the even-numbered lines in "My life closed twice before its close" are indented in Mrs. Todd's transcript (see Fig. 13). In the variorum the editor printed them flush even though in other instances—V1762, V1763, V1764, V1767 —he retained such indentation.

The only punctuation Mr. Johnson wished to reproduce from these transcripts was the punctuation first copied in ink, not the later additions in pencil, but his reproductions contain several errors. In "Death is like the insect" (V1716) the comma that he printed at the end of line 5 was not part of Mrs. Todd's first copy, but clearly a later addition in blue pencil.[48] The transcript for the poem "What mystery pervades a well" (V1400) had no punctuation in line 14 when Mrs. Todd first copied it. When preparing the poem for press, she added in pencil a dash which she later crossed out.[49] The variorum editor mistook the pencil for ink and retained the editorial dash.

The variorum printing of "How dare the robins sing" (V1724) has errors in both text and punctuation. Mrs. Todd's transcript, from which the variorum takes its text, originally had

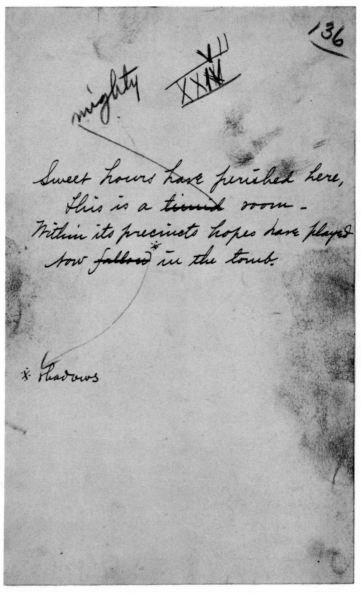

Fig. 16.—1896 printer's copy of V1767. By permission of the Amherst College Library.

a period following line 6.[50] In pencil Mrs. Todd later changed
this period to a comma which was carried over into the variorum.
When first transcribed, the word "bequeath" in line 12 had no
final *s*—as was often characteristic of Emily Dickinson's use of
the present, third person singular form of verbs. At the same
time that Mrs. Todd changed the period following line 6 to a
comma, she added an *s* to "bequeath" in order to have agreement between the verb and its singular subject. Mr. Johnson
apparently mistook pencil for ink, and "bequeath" incorrectly
appears as "bequeaths" in the variorum.[51] Finally, the variorum
text of this poem is marred by a misreading in line 15. The
printer's copy plainly reads "wrestled," while the variorum text
that derived from it reads "wrestles."[52]

Besides these errors, the variorum has a questionable handling
of the alternate readings in the poems reproduced from the
printer's copy. The editor does not explain what his practice was,
but when multiple readings were indicated within a line, one
above the other and usually bracketed, his pattern of choice for
the main text in the variorum was: V1738—top alternate;
V1740—bottom alternate, top alternate, bottom alternate; V1748
—bottom alternate, bottom alternate, bottom alternate, top
alternate; and V1400—bottom alternate, bottom alternate,
and top alternate.[53] His eight choices for the first three poems
were the same as those Mrs. Todd chose when editing the third
series (Figs. 17, 18, 19),[54] and one might conclude that Mr.
Johnson's policy was to follow Mrs. Todd's choices, although it
would mean that he was reproducing not just her copying, but
also her editing. But his three choices in the fourth poem
(V1400) were not the same as Mrs. Todd's (Fig. 20),[55] and
this fact suggests that the variorum editor, who claimed to be
making no critical choice among the alternate readings, was
simply inconsistent.[56] By later omitting all the notes and all the
alternate readings and printing only the main text from the
variorum, Mr. Johnson has made standard in the 1960 one-
volume edition versions that were achieved neither critically nor
even arbitrarily, but merely inconsistently.

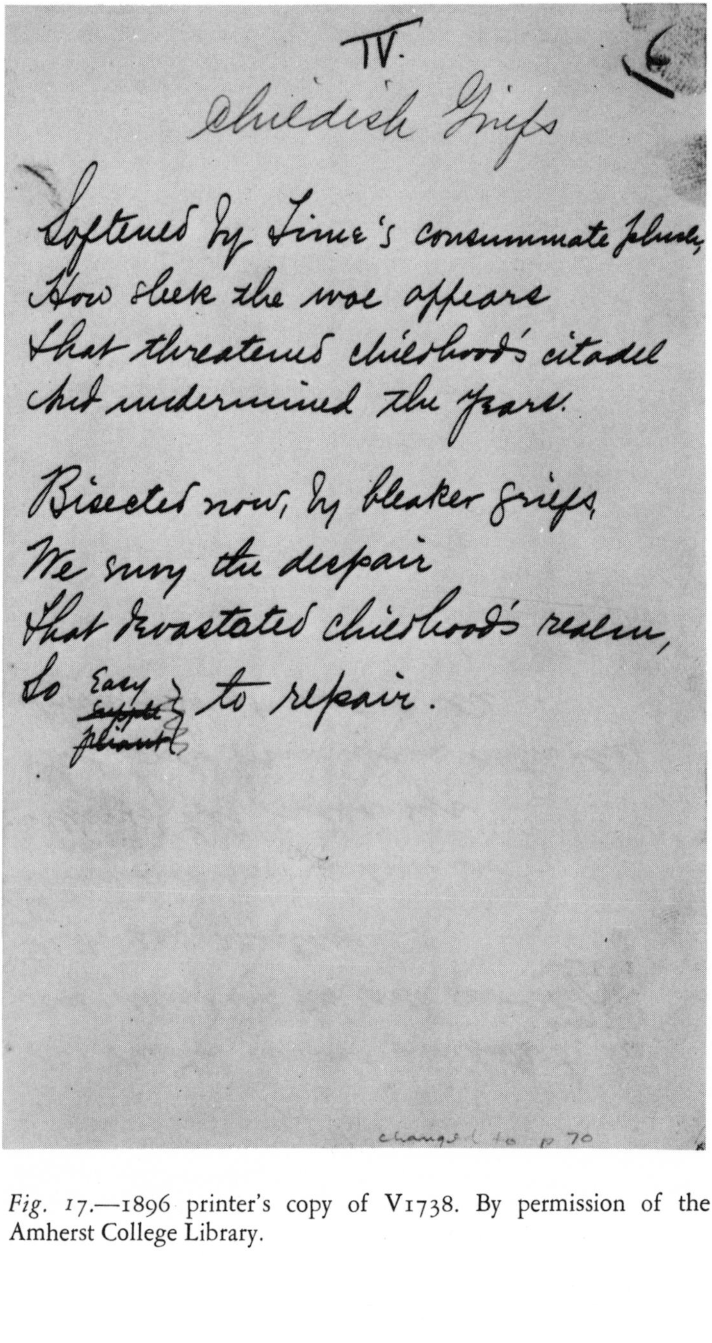

IV.

Childish Griefs

Softened by Time's consummate plush,
How sleek the woe appears
That threatened childhood's citadel
And undermined the years.

Bisected now, by bleaker griefs,
We envy the despair
That devastated childhood's realm,
So ~~supple~~ ~~pliant~~ Easy to repair.

changed to p 70

Fig. 17.—1896 printer's copy of V1738. By permission of the Amherst College Library.

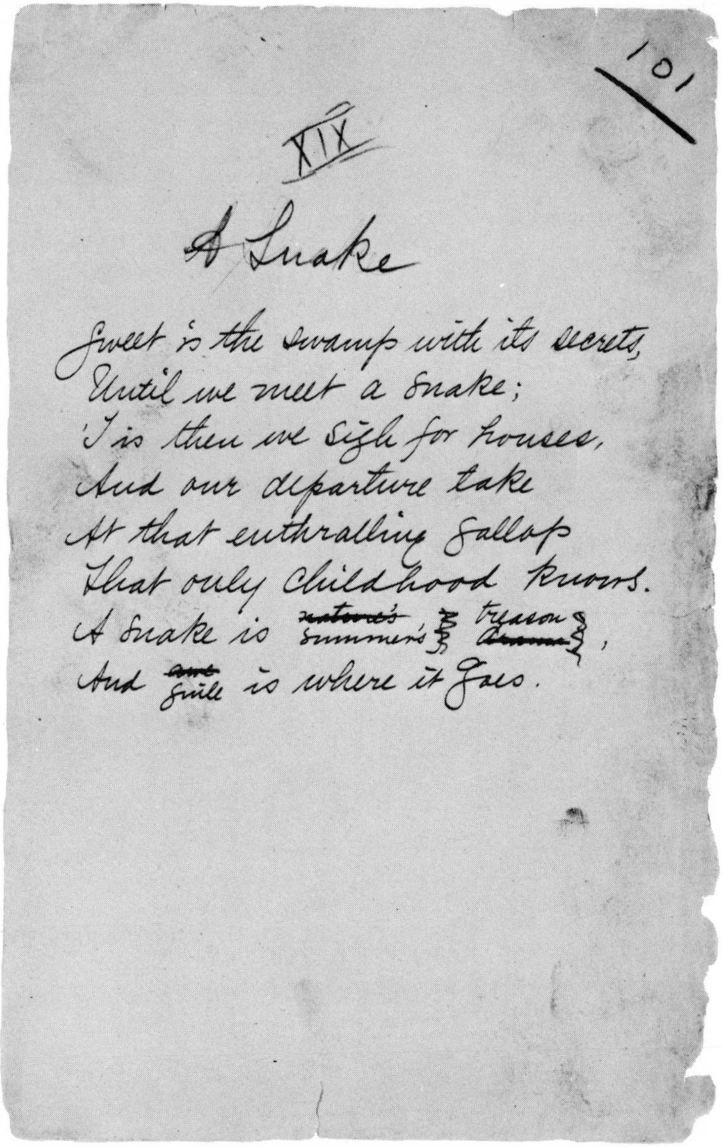

101

XIX

A Snake

Sweet is the swamp with its secrets,
Until we meet a snake;
'T is then we sigh for houses,
And our departure take
At that enthralling gallop
That only childhood knows.
A snake is summer's ~~nature's~~ treason,
And guile is where it goes.

Fig. 18.—1896 printer's copy of V1740. By permission of the Amherst College Library.

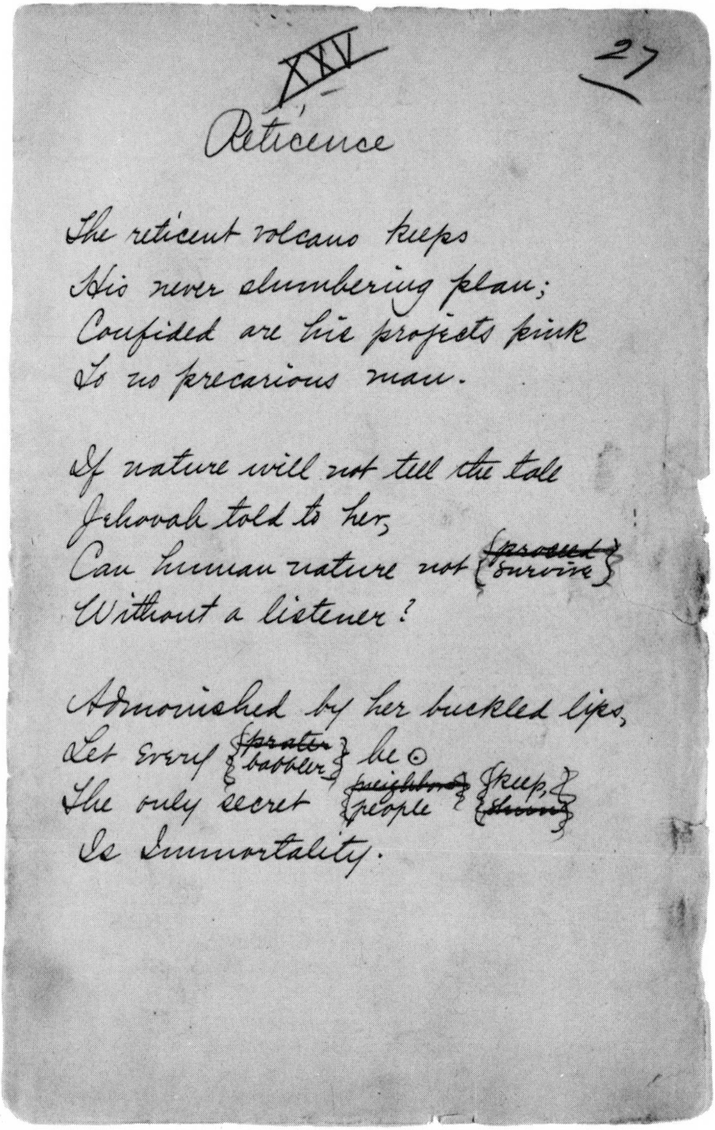

XXV

Reticence

The reticent volcano keeps
His never slumbering plan;
Confided are his projects pink
To no precarious man.

If nature will not tell the tale
Jehovah told to her,
Can human nature not {passed}{survive}
Without a listener?

Admonished by her buckled lips,
Let every {prater}{babbler} be ⊙
The only secret {neighbors}{people} {keep,}{known}
Is Immortality.

Fig. 19.—1896 printer's copy of V1748. By permission of the Amherst College Library.

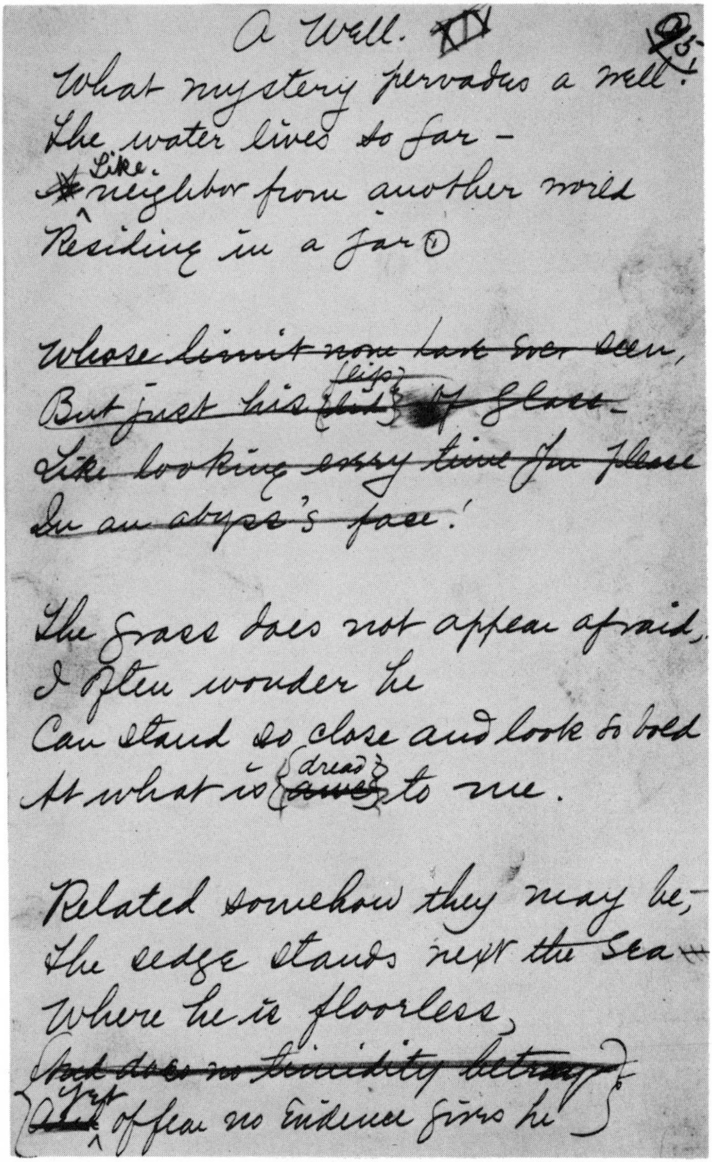

A Well. ~~XIV~~ 95

What mystery pervades a well!
The water lives so far –
~~A~~ Like neighbor from another world
Residing in a jar ①

~~Whose limit none have ever seen,~~
~~But just his {lid} {lips} of Glass –~~
~~Like looking every time you please~~
~~In an abyss's face!~~

The grass does not appear afraid,
I often wonder he
Can stand so close and look so bold
At what is {~~awe~~ dread} to me.

Related somehow they may be, –
The sedge stands next the sea –
Where he is floorless,
~~And does no timidity betray~~
~~And~~ Yet of fear no evidence gives he

Fig. 20.—1896 printer's copy (first page) of V1400. By permission of the Amherst College Library.

COLLATION OF MANUSCRIPTS

A collation of the texts in the variorum with the manuscripts that survive for poems in the third series shows the variorum to have several misreadings. In the manuscript for "I cried at Pity—not at Pain" (V588), the fifteenth line of the poem begins "As so and so" (Fig. 21) not "And so and so" as the variorum has it.[57] In Emily Dickinson's manuscript (Fig. 22)[58] for the poem "A sepal, petal, and a thorn" (V19), the

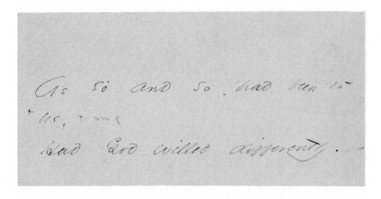

Fig. 21.—Holograph of lines 15–16 of V588. By permission of the Harvard College Library.

fourth line reads: "A Breeze—a'caper in the trees—". In the variorum the apostrophe is omitted from "a'caper" so that what was intended as a verb form modifying "Breeze" becomes an independent noun.[59]

The second stanza (lines 11–17) of "Dear March—Come in" (V1320) appears in the variorum in this manner:

I got your Letter, and the Birds—
The Maples never knew that you were coming—till I called
I declare—how Red their Faces grew—
But March, forgive me—and
All those Hills you left for me to Hue—   15
There was no Purple suitable—
You took it all with you—

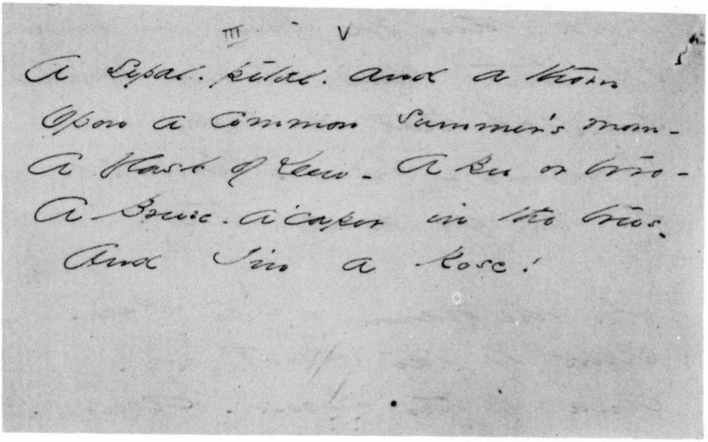

Fig. 22.—Holograph of V19. By permission of the Amherst College Library.

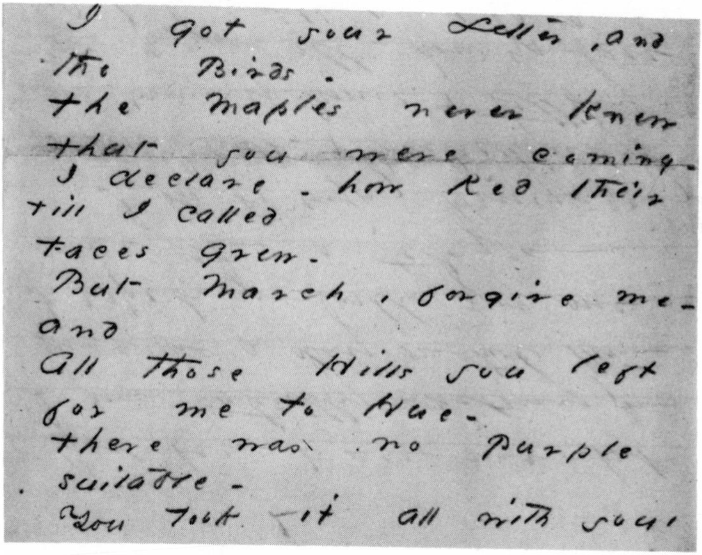

Fig. 23.—Holograph of lines 11–17 of V1320. By permission of the Amherst College Library.

According to the variorum, the text that Mrs. Todd published in the third series was not accurate since she omitted the phrase "till I called" from line 12. A careful look at the manuscript (Fig. 23),[60] however, substantiates her decision. The phrase "till I called" does not belong to line 12, but is an alternate reading for the first words of line 13: "I declare." In the manuscript Emily Dickinson has indicated this by placing the alternate reading below the other one, as she not infrequently did. Mrs. Todd was correct in omitting the phrase, and it should be taken out of the main text in the variorum.[61]

"We never know we go when we are going" (V1523) is another third series poem whose alternate readings are inadequately handled in the variorum. Figure 24 reproduces the manuscript, a semifinal draft jotted down on two scraps of paper that have been pinned together.[62] The final line (on the second scrap) originally read "And we accost no more—". Later Emily Dickinson added "we know" above "no more" and linked them within parentheses. In the variorum Mr. Johnson prints the final line as she first wrote it, and then he lists "we know" as an alternate reading for "no more." The two phrases, of course, are associated, but probably not in the manner that the variorum in-

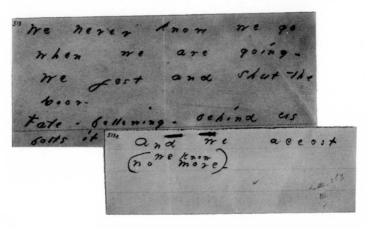

Fig. 24.—Holograph of V1523. By permission of the Amherst College Library.

dicates. If we follow the variorum listing, which interprets them as an either/or choice, and were to choose the alternate phrase, the final line would be nonsense: "And we accost we know." It was not Emily Dickinson's custom to draw lines around alternate suggestions; in this case she did not need them to indicate that the phrases were to be associated, for that is perfectly clear without the parentheses. The parentheses must have been used for another purpose: to indicate, not that one phrase is a substitute for the other, but that they go together. Emily Dickinson's substitute reading for the final line should be "we know no more."[63]

The third series poem "A Dew sufficed itself" (V1437) survives in a semifinal draft and four fair copies. According to Mr. Johnson's notes to the poem, the earliest copy (the semifinal draft) and the latest "are identical in text,"[64] yet the texts that he prints for the semifinal draft and fair copy IV differ. A collation of the variorum text of fair copy IV with the manuscript itself[65] discloses differences in the text of lines 3 and 7 as well as in the punctuation in eight other lines. In the printing style of the variorum, fair copy IV, reproduced in Figure 25, should be rendered:

> A Dew sufficed itself
> And satisfied a Leaf—
> And thought "how vast a destiny"—
> "How trivial is Life"!
>
> The Sun went out to work—   5
> The Day went out to play—
> But not again that Dew be seen
> By Physiognomy—
>
> Whether by Day abducted
> Or emptied by the Sun   10
> Into the Sea in passing—
> Eternally unknown—
>
> Attested to this Day
> That awful Tragedy
> By Transport's instability   15
> And Doom's celerity—

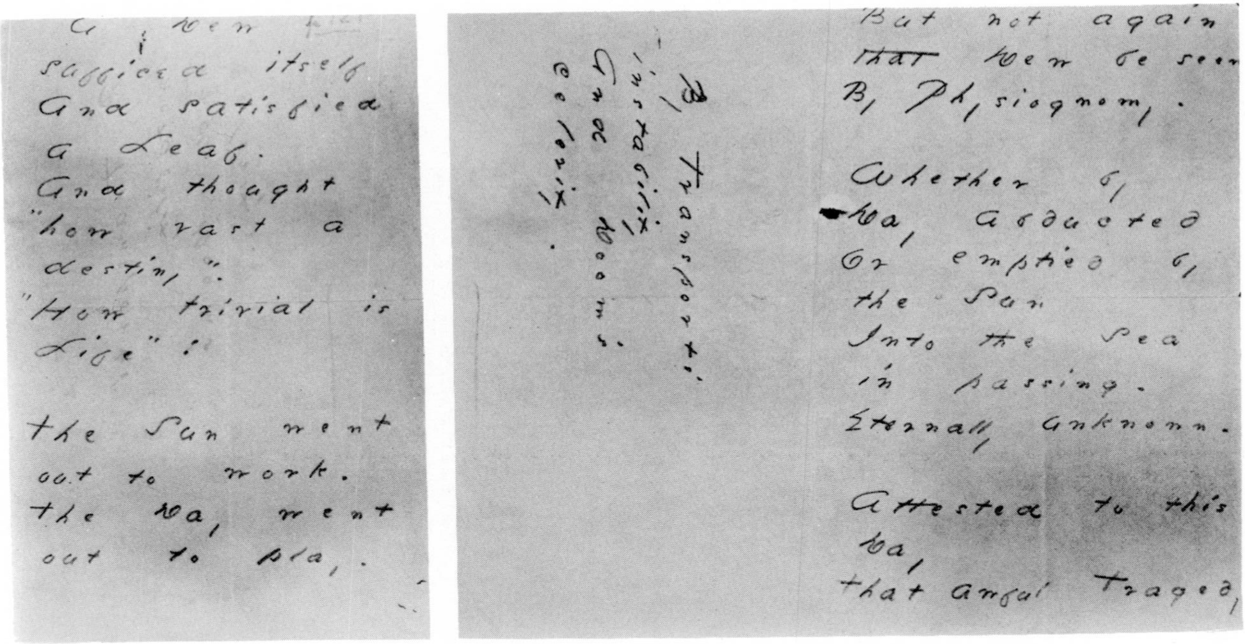

Fig. 25.—Holograph of V1437 (fair copy IV). By permission of the Wellesley College Library.

The variorum text for this copy incorrectly reads "felt" instead of "thought" in line 3 and "And" instead of "But" in line 7. Though doubt may be reasonable, "abducted" in line 9 should probably begin with a lower case letter instead of a capital. The variorum punctuation is erroneous in lines 1, 2, 4, 6, 8, 11, 12, and 16.

VARIANT VERSIONS, INCOMPLETE POEMS, AND OMISSIONS

Since many of Emily Dickinson's poems vary from copy to copy, the question When does a variant version become an independent poem? presents itself not only as a philosophical inquiry, but also as a practical problem in editing. The variorum policy was to group all variant versions, as versions not as separate poems, in the notes to the text chosen for principal representation. For example, the poet wrote a quatrain (V1619) on the dawn that, with the substitution of "herself" for the word "dawn" and the change of a single pronoun, served to express her reaction to the death of Helen Hunt Jackson. Strictly viewed, these versions may be separate poems, but some practical way of handling the large number of variants in Emily Dickinson's poetry was needed, and the variorum editor chose to print variants together, considering them versions of one poem.

Mr. Johnson, however, has departed from his policy with two poems from the third series, a discrepancy first noted by Jay Leyda in 1956.[66] He prints a variant of three lines in V342—

> The Aster—on the Hill
> Her everlasting fashion—set—
> And Covenant Gentians—frill—

as an independent poem numbered V331:

> While Asters—
> On the Hill—
> Their Everlasting fashions—set—
> And Covenant Gentians—Frill!

Four words differ between these two versions, two of the differences merely that between a singular and a plural noun. The variorum editor also prints a variant of the second stanza of V937—

> The thought behind, I strove to join
> Unto the thought before—
> But Sequence ravelled out of Sound
> Like Balls—upon a Floor.

as a different poem, numbered V992:

> The Dust behind I strove to join
> Unto the Disk before—
> But Sequence ravelled out of Sound
> Like Balls upon a Floor—

Here only two words differ in the two stanzas, and like the first pair, they should be printed together. The variorum notes to these four poems have references to the related poems, but in *Complete Poems* (1960), where the notes have been eliminated, the four variants stand alone, detached as though each had no closer relationship to other poems than a common author.[67]

The variorum has handled two other poems from the third series so that they now stand incomplete. The first, "To venerate the simple days" (V57), was discussed in detail in the preceding chapter. Its two stanzas became separated when Austin and/or Lavinia mutilated packet 80. The second stanza was subsequently lost, but not before Mrs. Todd made a transcript of the full poem which she published in the third series. In the variorum the editor noted that the 1896 text had a second stanza, but he gave principal representation to the surviving piece of manuscript containing the first stanza alone. Consequently, when the one-volume edition was published in 1960, "To venerate the simple days" was standardized as a one-stanza poem.

The second incomplete poem, also first noted by Mr. Leyda, is "On the Bleakness of my Lot" (V681).[68] The full manuscript, in this case, is extant and has two stanzas:

On the Bleakness of my Lot
Bloom I strove to raise—
Late—My Garden of a Rock—[69]
Yielded Grape—and Maise—

Soil of Flint, if steady tilled
Will refund the Hand—
Seed of Palm, by Lybian Sun
Fructified in Sand—

Emily Dickinson also made a copy of the last four lines and sent them to Sue, as she occasionally did. Mr. Johnson chose this single stanza for his principal representation in the variorum, placing the full copy in the notes. While the second stanza may stand alone, it follows naturally from the first, completes it, and together they form a unified poem of larger breadth. By eliminating the notes to the poems, the 1960 edition has arbitrarily settled half the poem as the complete version.

The variorum does not record a few extant manuscripts for third series poems. For "We like March" (V1213) there are two in addition to those cited by Mr. Johnson. One is a fragment containing the two concluding lines of the poem:

With the Blue Birds buccaneering
On his British sky[70]

The other unrecorded manuscript for this poem is signed "March—"; it gives the final stanza in full:

News is He of all the Others—
Bold it were to die
With the Blue Birds buccaneering
On his British Sky—[71]

Finally, the variorum does not list a surviving fragment for the poem "Not with a Club, the Heart is broken" (V1304). Containing only the thirteenth line of the poem, the fragment reads: "Shame need not crouch."[72]

SUMMARY

The variorum did not use the 1896 printer's copy and the large store of surviving transcripts as fully as possible. One can show that "Not any higher stands the Grave" (V1256) was published in 1896 from packet 93, not from Higginson's copy, that "Few, yet enough" (V1596) had another manuscript, that "Savior! I've no one else to tell" (V217) was not sent to Sue, and that an authentic variant version of the poem "Of Tolling Bell I ask the cause" (V947) once existed in Emily Dickinson's manuscript though all we now have is Mrs. Todd's transcript of it. One can also show that the spelling of "befel" in the poem "My life closed twice before its close" (V1732) may not have been Emily Dickinson's and that the alternate reading ("disclose") to the same poem was probably not hers, but Mrs. Todd's.

The variorum erred in recounting the publishing history of "Sweet hours have perished here" (V1767), stating that it first appeared in *Complete Poems* (1924), instead of in the third series (1896), and, as a result, it included one of Mrs. Todd's editorial alterations ("mighty") as part of Emily Dickinson's text while omitting one of the poet's alternate readings ("fallow"). In the case of "Who has not found the Heaven—below" (V1544) the variorum correctly indicated that the poem had been published in the third series, but did not record another of Emily Dickinson's alternate readings found on the printer's copy ("livery"). The editor did properly go to the 1896 printer's copy for texts of some eighteen poems whose holographs could not be found, but in some of them he improperly or inconsistently reproduced stanza arrangement (V1732), punctuation (V1716, V1400, V1724), and textual readings (V1724—"bequeaths" for "bequeath" and "wrestles" for "wrestled"). The variorum, moreover, has a questionable handling of the alternate readings for these poems.

When the variorum texts for third series poems were collated with Emily Dickinson's holographs, several misreadings came to light. In "I cried at Pity—not at Pain" (V588) the fifteenth line incorrectly reads "And so and so" instead of "As so and so." In the fourth line of "A sepal, petal, and a thorn" (V19) the editor overlooked the apostrophe in "a'caper," inadvertently turning a dependent modifier into an independent noun. The variorum text of "A Dew sufficed itself" (V1437, fair copy IV) proved to be faulty in line 3 ("felt" for "thought") and in line 7 ("And" for "But"), at the same time that it presented faulty punctuation in eight other lines. In "Dear March—Come in" (V1320) Mr. Johnson apparently misunderstood the alternate choices ("till I called" and "I declare") as he also did in "We never know we go when we are going" (V1523).

Twice the variorum printed incomplete variants of larger poems as full poems themselves (V331 and V992), while in two other instances (V57 and V681) it gave principal representation to one-stanza copies of two-stanza poems, thereby arbitrarily settling half the poems as the complete versions in later editions. This study cited a few manuscripts that the variorum did not record, though none was of large significance and some were not available until after Mr. Johnson had finished working on the variorum. Although the focus here was not on punctuation and capitalization, a few such errors came to light in the course of the discussion.

The third series contained less than 10 per cent of Emily Dickinson's total canon and is probably not a valid sample from which to predict the general accuracy of the variorum—if for no other reason than that it has a surviving printer's copy to complicate the editorial procedure while the other poems do not. But the variorum, it should be said, stands in need of revision.

EPILOGUE

When Mrs. Todd returned from Japan in October of 1896, the third series had already been published. A few reviewers praised the volume, but there was not much critical acclaim. Even the enthusiasm of purchasers, which had previously outstripped the enthusiasm of reviewers, had subsided. The *Letters of Emily Dickinson* (1894) had not sold well; now the third series of poems moved slowly too. The temporary Dickinson vogue was over, and the fame that belongs to Emily Dickinson escaped her for a while longer. Beginning with large promise, the second phase in the nineteenth-century editing of Emily Dickinson's poetry (1891–96) ended with disappointment.

But the disappointment was not merely commercial, nor did this phase in the editing end because of commercial failure. Mrs. Todd stopped working on the poems because of difficulties with Lavinia. Before his death, Austin had insisted to Lavinia that in part payment for services Mrs. Todd should share the royalties from the *Letters* and should be deeded a strip of land that adjoined the Todd home lot. Lavinia agreed to both proposals with great reluctance, and when Austin died in 1895 only the contract for the *Letters* had been negotiated. Lavinia delayed further, but before Mrs. Todd left for Japan in 1896, Lavinia signed the deed transferring the property to her.

By the time Mrs. Todd returned to Amherst, Lavinia had changed her mind, and less than a month later she filed suit to recover the property, alleging that she had not known the paper she had signed was a deed, but rather an agreement that no house should be built on the land. Lavinia's case was weak, her testimony contradictory, but she was awarded the decision even so. The Todds appealed to the Supreme Judicial Court of Massachusetts in the hope of a reversal. The higher court sustained the decision, however, on the grounds that the judge who had presided at the trial had had the opportunity to see and hear the witnesses while the higher court had not. Having twice lost court decisions, Mrs. Todd returned the land, but having been publicly accused of fraud by Lavinia, she renounced their friendship and refused to work further on Emily Dickinson's manuscripts.[73] The editing ceased altogether, for Lavinia herself was not capable of handling them, and Susan Dickinson, perhaps the only other capable person around, was hostile. *Poems, Third Series* (1896) was the last of the nineteenth-century volumes.

CHAPTER IV

The Present: The Question of a Readers' Edition

The break between Mrs. Todd and Lavinia Dickinson because of the lawsuit was complete, and with the break came the division of the manuscripts. Lavinia had possession of packets 1–38, 40, Mrs. Todd of packets 80–95 and also a great many loose poems.[1] Mrs. Todd packed her share away, where they remained for many years. Sometime after Lavinia's death in 1899, Susan Dickinson gained possession of Lavinia's share, and in 1914 the poet's niece, Martha Dickinson Bianchi, began issuing additions to the published canon. *The Single Hound* appeared in 1914, *Further Poems* in 1929, and *Unpublished Poems* in 1935.

The Single Hound (1914), however, did not come from Lavinia's manuscripts. It published poems that Emily Dickinson had sent across the hedge to Sue and her family, and generally it presented them in a faithful text. By 1929 Lavinia's manuscripts had been located and their importance recognized. *Further Poems* (1929) and *Unpublished Poems* (1935), edited with the assistance of Alfred Leete Hampson, derived mainly from Lavinia's packets. These two volumes, however, contained numerous misreadings of the manuscripts as well as conscious attempts to satisfy a new public taste by making Emily Dickinson's form even more eccentric than it was.[2] After each of these individual installments, Mrs. Bianchi and Mr. Hampson brought out a "complete" edition of the poetry by taking the three nineteenth-century editions—including many of the alterations and errors—and adding to them the newer installments. In 1943 Mrs. Bianchi died, the last of the Dickinson line. In 1945 Millicent Todd Bingham, the last of the Todd line, published *Bolts of Melody,* over six hundred unpublished poems garnered from the manuscripts and transcripts that had lain among her mother's papers since the 1890's.

The text of the poems in *Bolts of Melody* was generally accurate,[3] but the volume contained only a part of Emily Dickinson's full canon. The rest was accessible only in undependable versions, either from the nineteenth-century editions or from Mrs. Bianchi's collections. As Emily Dickinson came to be an object of study by the professional student of literature, well-known scholars and critics lamented the restrictions imposed by the published condition of the poems. R. P. Blackmur, in 1937, scoffed at the available volumes:

> The disarray of Emily Dickinson's poems is the great obvious fact about them as they multiply from volume to volume—I will not say from edition to edition, for they have never been edited.[4]

At mid-century *Bolts of Melody* was the only collection that Blackmur might have called an edition.[5] The great need was for a trustworthy variorum edition of the complete canon.

At mid-century, too, the opportunity for such an edition came. In 1950 Alfred Leete Hampson, the heir of Mrs. Bianchi, sold the Dickinson materials to Harvard University. Through the purchase agreement, Harvard claimed ownership and right of possession of all the manuscripts, including those Millicent Todd Bingham had gained from her mother. Harvard's claim has not stood, and Mrs. Bingham returned her mother's share of the manuscripts to Amherst, depositing them in the Amherst College Library, while Lavinia's share of the manuscripts, augmented by those Emily Dickinson sent to the family across the hedge, has come to rest at the Houghton Library. While Harvard was contesting her ownership of the manuscripts, Mrs. Bingham allowed Thomas H. Johnson access to them, and with the full complement of the manuscripts available to him, Mr. Johnson published *The Poems of Emily Dickinson* (1955), the three-volume variorum edition. Five years later, in 1960, he brought out a one-volume readers' edition, *The Complete Poems of Emily Dickinson.*

THE MECHANICS OF THE VERSE

The variorum tried to make Emily Dickinson's poetry available as she wrote it. The representation, however, is not exact because printing is itself a misrepresentation of the texts as they exist in manuscript. Though this is a problem of all printing, it is more acute with the Dickinson texts, in which the difficulties of rendering the poems in print are compounded by the poet's handwriting and individual mode of punctuation. Her peculiarities in shaping letters make distinguishing between small and large ones difficult, size frequently being the only distinction. In manuscript, as Charles R. Anderson has illustrated, the famous poem "Safe in their Alabaster Chambers" (V216) has four sizes of the letter *s*;[6] standardizing them into either upper or lower case type will be an editorial construction upon what the poet wrote. With her punctuation Emily Dickinson was lavish and unorthodox. She used commas and periods, but commonly she depended upon a mark of various lengths resembling a dash that tilts up or down as frequently as it is level. Because of her handwriting, it is often difficult to tell a comma from a dash and a dash from a lengthened period. Such punctuation cannot be reproduced exactly in type.

The mechanics of the many poems and letters Colonel Higginson received from Emily Dickinson so baffled him that when later asked to serve as her editor, he refused to work on the manuscripts of the poems. Mrs. Todd had to make copies before he would edit them. In an article in the *Atlantic* (1891), Higginson, speaking of his letters from Emily Dickinson, compared their mechanics with the poems':

> Of punctuation there was little; she used chiefly dashes, and it has been thought better, in printing these letters, as with her poems, to give them the benefit in this respect of the ordinary usages; and so with her habit as to capitalization . . . in which she followed the Old English and present German method of thus distinguishing every noun substantive.[7]

Higginson's failure to work closely with the manuscripts of the poems perhaps led him astray, for his explanation that Emily Dickinson capitalized every noun is incorrect. She did not capitalize every noun—there are many, many without capitals—while she did at various times capitalize every other one of the traditional parts of speech.

Mrs. Todd, whose familiarity with the manuscripts was much larger than Higginson's, explained that "all important words began with capitals,"[8] and her explanation has more merit than his, for importance and capitalization often do coincide. But important words are frequently without capitals, while words of lesser significance, articles for example, have them. Moreover, Emily Dickinson's capitalization is not restricted to the beginnings of words. Majuscules may also come medially and finally.

If the early editors did not agree on the significance of Emily Dickinson's mechanics, most twentieth-century commentators are not in full harmony either. Many, though, agree in various ways with Mrs. Todd that the capitals indicate stress or importance. John Crowe Ransom, a respected spokesman for this view, sees them as "a way of conferring dignity upon . . . poetic objects, or as a mythopoetic device, to push them a little further into the fertile domain of myth."[9] Charles R. Anderson believes Ransom's to be the most fruitful conjecture about the capitals; as for the punctuation, Mr. Anderson, following ideas of R. P. Blackmur and Austin Warren, regards it as "an attempt to create a new system of musical notation for reading her verse."[10] More recently Edith Perry Stamm has taken an inge-

nious slant in which she argues that the punctuation was not will-
ful eccentricity, nor simply musical notation, but rather rhetorical or elocutionary marks which Emily had learned at the
Amherst Academy, that they indicate voice inflection—monotone, rising inflection, falling inflection, and a combination of
rising and falling—and that "Dickinson's 'eccentric' punctuation, then, is simply meant to direct the reading of her verse."[11]

There are several objections to Miss Stamm's theory. In the
systems of elocution to which she refers, the marks are placed
above the words, not after them as Emily Dickinson has done.
Miss Stamm anticipated this argument by explaining away
Emily Dickinson's placement as a fusion of functions that "may
indicate a grammatical stop as well as rhetorical inflection."[12]
She also anticipated the objection that the punctuation varies
from copy to copy of the same poem. This fact, she says, should
not cause alarm, "for certainly no two readings of the same
poem, even by the same person, will ever be quite the same—
such is the nature of poetry."[13] Has not Miss Stamm here argued against the value of her own theory? If it is the nature of
poetry that no two readings will ever be the same, why should
a modern reader of Emily Dickinson's poetry be interested in
her unique renditions? They cannot govern his own, they cannot
"direct the reading of her verse"—if such is the nature of
poetry. Moreover, if there is no consistency in Emily Dickinson's intent, of what other value are these "elocutionary
marks"? To an editor seeking authority, not inconsistency, they
appear to have none. To the biographer or the curious, they
would be, if properly dated, merely the historical record of a
passing performance.

Theodora Ward, associate editor of the *Letters of Emily
Dickinson* (1958), who also assisted Mr. Johnson with the
poems, replied to Miss Stamm's article. Having worked on
Dickinson manuscripts for over twenty years, Mrs. Ward explained that the manner of using the punctuation marks varied
in the different periods of Emily Dickinson's life—they were
used most heavily during the years of emotional crisis—but that

in any one period the same marks could be found in letters as well as poems. If, as Miss Stamm suggests, Emily Dickinson's punctuation is "meant to direct the reading of her verse," it must serve a similar function with her letters. One letter Emily Dickinson wrote to Colonel Higginson in 1862 at the height of her overwhelming emotional crisis contained twenty-eight of her characteristic punctuation marks. "It is hard," Mrs. Ward rightly contends, "to imagine Emily urgently asking for help and at the same time dictating to her correspondent how to read her letter to an audience."[14] To this criticism Miss Stamm replied that the letters, too, were poetical.[15]

What then is the significance of Emily Dickinson's punctuation—and of her capitalization? With the exception of Mrs. Ward, most recent commentators, basing their theories mainly on the variorum rendering, have not worked closely with the manuscripts. Familiarity with the manuscripts should show that the capitals and the dashes were merely a habit of handwriting and that Emily Dickinson used them inconsistently, without system. Part of the evidence for such a view has come to the surface in the preceding discussion. The capitals, it was pointed out, were used on nouns, but not every noun, at times on every other part of speech, and on important and unimportant words alike. Emily Dickinson's capitalization, if followed literally, would come in the middle and at the end of words as well as at the beginning. Frequently several autograph copies of the same poem exist, each with variant punctuation and capitalization. The famous poem "Success is counted sweetest" (V67), for example, has three fair copies. Though the text is identical in all three, the punctuation and capitalization differ. Clearly, what with Emily Dickinson was a habit of handwriting was not a consistent one.

That the capitals and dashes were merely habits of handwriting without special significance is also shown by the poet's using them not only for poems but for letters too. As Mrs. Ward's reply to Miss Stamm demonstrated, any special theory about Emily Dickinson's mechanics will have to fit both poems and

letters. Any such theory will also have to account for other instances, for Emily Dickinson used her characteristic habits of
writing whenever she wrote. Examples have survived wherein
she copied passages from Swinburne, Emerson, George Herbert,
and the Bible.[16] In these copies she translated type into her own
peculiar writing, complete with capitals and dashes where they
had not been. Household notes,[17] at least one shopping list,[18]
and several recipes[19] have survived to illustrate her handwriting
on more domestic concerns. The recipe for coconut cake
gained from Mrs. Carmichael, an Amherst neighbor, is reproduced in Figure 26.[20]

Emily Dickinson's copy of the recipe exhibits her characteristic capitals and dashes. If we follow John Crowe Ransom's
theory, the capitals are Emily's "way of conferring dignity"
upon the ingredients of Mrs. Carmichael's cake, or are her
"mythopoetic device" for pushing Butter, Flour, 6 Eggs, and a
Cocoa Nut (grated) into "the fertile domain of myth." At the
same time, according to Charles R. Anderson, we are asked to
use the punctuation here as "a new system of musical notation
for reading" the recipe. Or, applying Miss Stamm's theory,
Emily Dickinson has not only got the recipe, but has indicated
how one is to declaim it, though in this case since the dashes are
nearly level, a monotone should be used—even on Mrs. Carmichael's name. The absurdity of such theories argues strongly
that the poet's capitals and dashes are merely a habitual part
of her manner of writing. The argument is supported further
when the recipe is turned over (Fig. 27) and it is seen that on
the verso Emily Dickinson's draft of the poem "The Things
that never can come back, are several" (V1515), in the writing of the same period as the recipe, exhibits identical characteristics. Poems, letters, copied passages, household notes, shopping
lists, and recipes—all have the capitals and dashes, for Emily
Dickinson used them whenever she wrote.

In propounding her theory, Miss Stamm was concerned to
divest Emily Dickinson of eccentricity by showing that there was
a well-known system informing her punctuation, yet as Mrs.

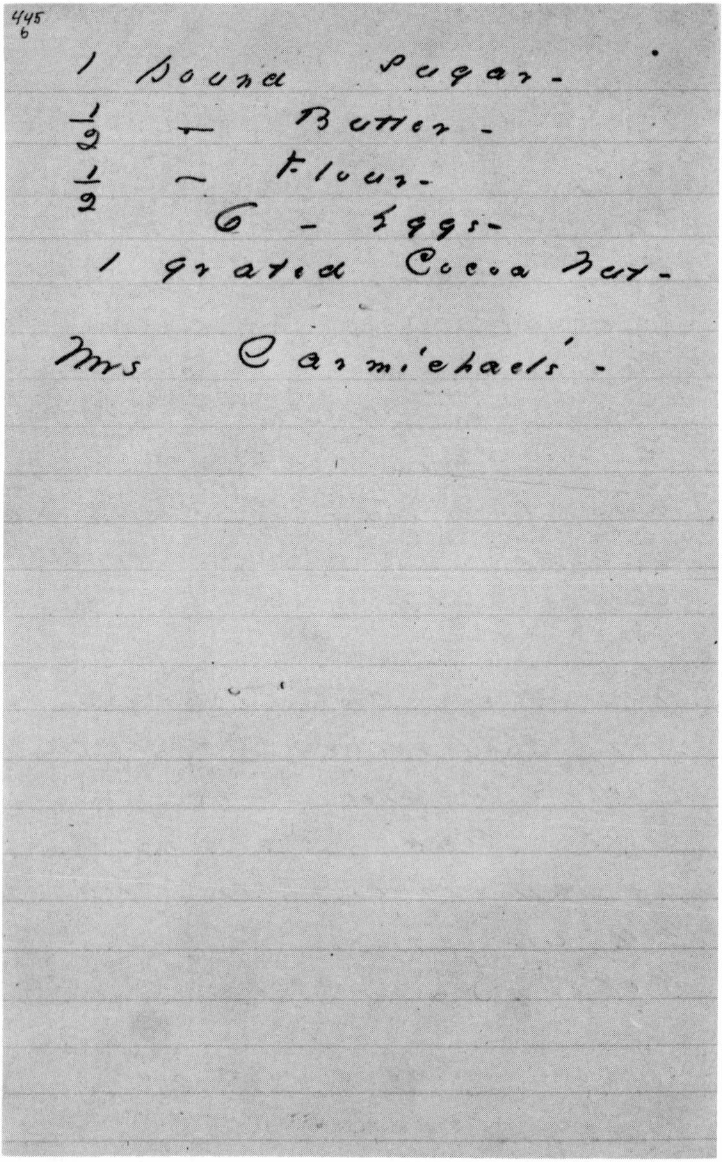
445
6

1 pound Sugar –
½ – Butter –
½ – Flour –
6 – Eggs –
1 grated Cocoa Nut –

Mrs Carmichael's –

Fig. 26.—Emily Dickinson's copy of Mrs. Carmichael's recipe. By permission of the Amherst College Library.

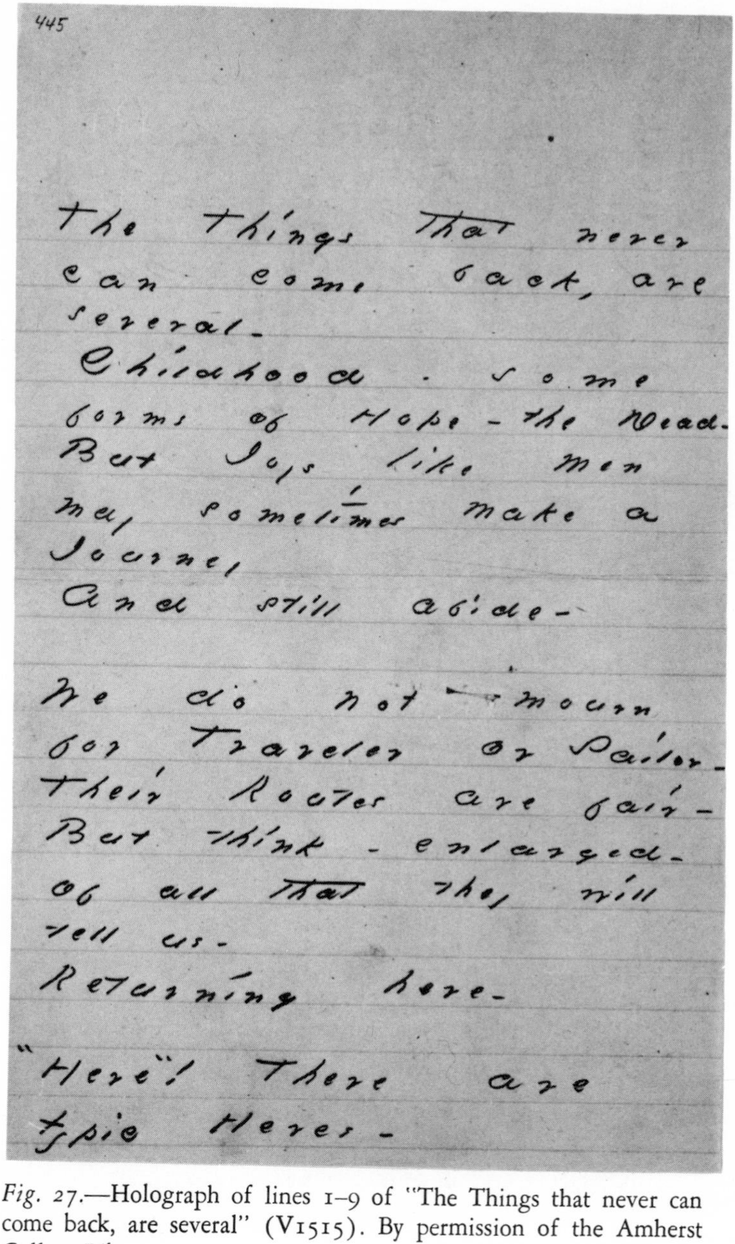

445

The things that never
can come back, are
several -
Childhood - some
forms of Hope - the Dead -
But Joys - like men
may sometimes make a
Journey
And still abide -

We do not mourn
for Traveler or Sailor -
Their Routes are fair -
But think - enlarged -
Of all that they will
tell us -
Returning here -

"Here"! There are
typic Heres -

Fig. 27.—Holograph of lines 1–9 of "The Things that never can come back, are several" (V1515). By permission of the Amherst College Library.

Ward has shown, this theory would make her odder yet. If by eccentricity we mean inconsistency, Emily Dickinson was eccentric. But viewed in another perspective, she was participating in the fashions of her times, for a free use of capitals, but more particularly of dashes, is frequently found in nineteenth-century handwriting, particularly that of women. Mrs. Todd, for example, used capitals inside of words and out, and the free use of dashes can be documented from Emily Dickinson's own friends.[21]

One box in the Amherst Collection contains some of the correspondence associated with the nineteenth-century editing of the Dickinson poems, including at least thirty letters by twenty-four different writers in which the dash was used in place of conventional punctuation.[22] In another box there are several by William Hayes Ward, the learned editor of the *Independent,* and his sister, Susan Hayes Ward, to Mrs. Todd regarding the publication of some of the poems. It is significant that in their handwritten letters the Wards used the dash in place of other punctuation, yet in the instances in which the letters were typed, they observed conventional usage.[23] Thomas Johnson apparently saw Emily Dickinson's case as parallel. Noting her "especially capricious" use of the dash, Mr. Johnson said in the variorum that

> quite properly such "punctuation" can be omitted in later editions, and the spelling and capitalization regularized, as surely she would have expected had her poems been published in her lifetime. Here however the literal rendering is demanded.[24]

Emily Dickinson had translated George Herbert's verses from standard type into the peculiarities of her handwriting;[25] conversely, she would, according to Mr. Johnson, have expected her peculiarities to be changed in the translation of her poems into type. The objective of the variorum, however, was a literal rendering. The change should come in later editions.

While inconsistent, "capricious," "eccentric," Emily Dickinson's capitals and dashes occasionally have discernible functions. Habits are usually not consciously controlled, but on occasion they may be. Aware of the idiosyncrasies of her handwriting, Emily Dickinson compensated for them at times when she felt confusion might result. There are instances in which she capitalized words, not because they began lines or even sentences, but because they indicated grammatical units when her dashes alone might have failed to. In lines 3 and 4 of V19 the poet capitalized three *A*'s to show parallel structure:

> A sepal, petal, and a thorn
> Upon a common summer's morn—
> A flask of Dew—A Bee or two—
> A Breeze—a caper in the trees—
> And I'm a Rose!

The *a* before "caper" in the fourth line is not capitalized because the phrase it belongs to is not grammatically parallel to the preceding three. In the manuscript, as we have seen (see Fig. 22), there is an apostrophe between "a" and "caper" that was not printed in the variorum. The apostrophe is important, however, for it signifies that together they form not a noun and its article, but a verb form that modifies "Breeze." Thus the full phrase "A breeze a'caper in the trees" is the third of the parallel grammatical units—as Emily Dickinson's punctuation and capitalization function to indicate.

In regularizing Emily Dickinson's texts, an editor must be sensitive to any help that the poet's handwriting can give him. And he will ideally work from the manuscripts themselves. One twentieth-century commentator, Austin Warren, suggested that for a readers' text all punctuation be omitted, a practice he believed would in no case "obscure the comprehension of her poetry."[26] A German critic, Kurt Oppens, in editing Emily Dickinson's texts for an article, followed a method similar to Mr. Warren's suggestion. His English version of V297, produced from the variorum edition but with most of the capitals and punctuation of the variorum omitted, reads:

> It's like the light
> A fashionless delight
> It's like the bee
> A dateless melody
>
> It's like the woods   5
> Private like the breeze
> Phraseless—yet it stirs
> The proudest trees
>
> It's like the morning
> Best when it's done   10
> And the everlasting clocks
> Chime noon[27]

By looking at the manuscript for the poem, reproduced in Figure 28, one can see that Emily Dickinson did not capitalize the word "like" in lines 1, 3, 5, and 9, but that she did so in line 6. Conscious that confusion could occur in line 6, she used the capital to signal that "Like" begins a separate grammatical unit: "Private" goes with the preceding line, while "Like the Breeze" goes with "Phraseless" in the next.

Contrary to Mr. Warren's belief, Mr. Oppens has made the syntax misleading by removing the punctuation and capitals and not substituting others. Mr. Oppens himself errs in reading "Private" with line 6 instead of line 5. His German paraphrase of the stanza reads: "es ist wie die Wälder, in sich beschlossen wie der Wind, sprachlos, und doch bewegt es die stolzesten Bäume."[28] (Or in translation: "it is like the woods, private like the breeze, speechless . . . .") Mr. Warren's suggestion, as Charles R. Anderson has said, is "more an evasion than a solution" of the problem of a readers' text.[29] To meet the difficulties of such a text, the editor will have to work over the manuscripts in a sensitive endeavor to determine where amid Emily Dickinson's inconsistency he can find clues to help him along.

The task is difficult, but possible. The only significant attempt at a punctuated text was made by the English poet James Reeves,[30] but his edition is small, it is based on the variorum not on the manuscripts, and it contains errors—as when he puts a question mark after the third line of "A narrow Fellow in the

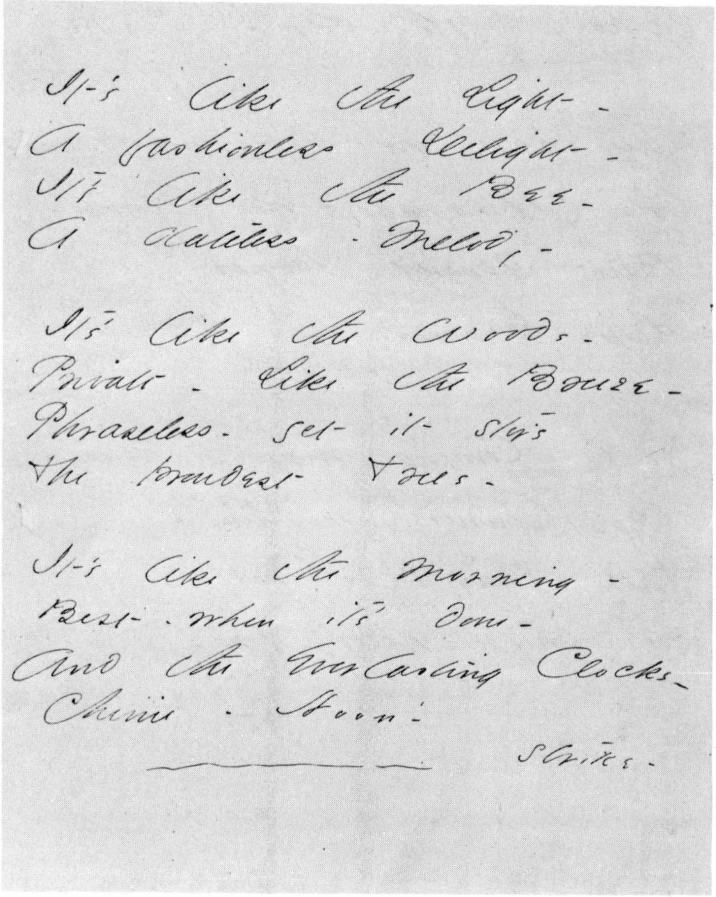

Fig. 28.—Holograph of "It's like the Light" (V297). By permission of the Harvard College Library.

Grass" (V986).[31] Mr. Johnson had the opportunity to produce such a text in 1960 when he published the one-volume edition, *The Complete Poems of Emily Dickinson.* He corrected misspellings (*visiter, Febuary*) and misplaced apostrophes (*does'nt, it's* for *its*), but he allowed the punctuation and capitalization used in the variorum to remain unchanged. Newton Arvin, for one, declared that "it is simply destructive of poetic pleasure" to read poem after poem punctuated in Emily Dickinson's eccentric manner.[32] And indeed her lavish use of capitals and the dash can annoy: "Departed—to the Judgment" (V524), a poem of only thirty-two words, has eighteen dashes and twenty capitals, and the poem " 'Twas the old—road—through pain" (V344), exhibiting a total of forty-four dashes, has nineteen of them within a seven-line stanza. Since the mechanics of the verse, like that of the letters, shopping lists, and recipes, is mainly a habit of her handwriting, an editor is needed to produce, not as a substitute for the variorum but as an addition to it, a readers' text whose capitalization and punctuation conform to modern usage. The task yet remains to be done.

THE TEXT

An editor of Emily Dickinson soon encounters a more difficult problem than the mechanics of her verse. One of the first requirements of a scholarly edition is to provide a text that represents as exactly as possible the author's final intention for the work. The usual practice is to collate the editions in which the author is known to have intervened or may have done so. From the collation the author's final intention may be hypothesized and a basic text chosen or constructed accordingly. In general, an editor now chooses the earliest authorized edition as a basic text and, from the collation with other editions, incorporates into it variants that can be shown to have later authority.[33] Scholarly editions are concerned only with authors' sanctioned texts, preferably the latest, in order to make their works available "as these artists intended them for their public."[34]

With Emily Dickinson we do not have the guidance of this principle, for she never willingly committed herself to print, nor even prepared her poems for publication. Publication, she wrote to Colonel Higginson, is as "foreign to my thought, as Firmament to Fin."[35] According to one poem (V709), it is "the Auction / Of the Mind of Man" ("so foul a thing"), and no human spirit should be reduced to "Disgrace of Price." But certain poems on fame and the famous poem "This is my letter to the World" (V441) suggest that at times she thought intently about gaining a larger audience, and some critics have conjectured a frustrated desire to publish.[36] There is, however, a large difference between frustrated desire and active intention when it comes to the practicalities of editing her texts. What Emily Dickinson's intention was concerning the fate of her poems after her death, if she herself really knew, perished at her death.

We cannot, then, publish Emily Dickinson's poems on the basis of her express intention. If we were to read the poems as her sanction gave us leave (assuming that she even sanctions our reading them), each reader would have to go directly to her manuscripts. A printed edition is clearly necessary, but the preparation of such a volume must be based on some principle other than the usual one. The purpose of the present variorum edition was to provide, within the limitations of print, a complete literal rendering of the poems, giving every version and every variant both in manuscript and in print for every poem. The problem of selection was thus set aside—and along with it the need of authorial intention as a criterion. We can see that finality was not a basic criterion when we learn that Mr. Johnson generally chose the earliest fair copy of each poem for principal representation.[37] He did so to establish an orderly chronology and to facilitate the printing of variants that were later.[38]

By giving a complete literal rendering, Mr. Johnson returned the poems to the manuscript states in which they were when Mrs. Todd first began to work upon them in the late 1880's. Each of the three manuscript states—worksheets, semifinal drafts, and even fair copies—lacks the sanction of authorial final intention. Worksheets obviously cannot claim it; they are merely first inspirations jotted in pencil on any available piece of paper. The poems generally remained in this preliminary state unless reworked into either a semifinal draft or a fair copy and incorporated into the packets. The semifinal drafts, according to Mr. Johnson, total "some three hundred,"[39] including such well-known poems as "I taste a liquor never brewed" (V214), "The Soul selects her own Society" (V303), "If you were coming in the Fall" (V511), "Mine—by the Right of the White Election!" (V528), "The Brain, within it's Groove" (V556), "I asked no other thing" (V621), "I cannot live with You" (V640), "You left me—Sire—two Legacies" (V644), and "Pain—has an Element of Blank" (V650). Semifinal drafts are unfinished in that the poet never made up her mind about her own suggested readings. She carefully copied these poems into the packets, placing in the margins or between lines such words as she was still considering, and noting with little crosses the corresponding points within the lines of the poems.[40] "Semifinal drafts," Mr. Johnson says in his introduction to the variorum, "unless she herself redacted them into fair copies, must always remain unfinished."[41]

In September 1951, when he had been at work upon the Dickinson manuscripts for a year, Mr. Johnson read a paper before the English Institute on the textual problems he was encountering. In the paper he explained why he gives up the semifinal drafts to an eternal limbo. Since there is rarely an indication of preference on these drafts themselves, Mr. Johnson tried to find other ways of determining the author's intention:

> In one instance I thought she herself had provided a solution. One of the poems which she copied into a packet had several suggested readings for eight different words in the course of the five stanzas, but with no indication of her choice. . . . Then I found the same poem included in a letter to Higginson with choices made in every instance. Here, then, seemed proof that she had established her final version. But in another letter to another correspondent, written at substantially the same time, she has included the same poem—also evidently a final version—wherein she adopted six of the choices made in the Higginson letter, but selected two from among her variants in the remaining instances. If any conclusion is to be drawn from this citation, it would seem to be that there are no *final* versions of the poems for which she allowed alternate readings to stand in the packets.[42]

The poet would occasionally underline marginal suggestions as if to indicate her choices, "but," in Mr. Johnson's words, "later fair copies of such poems are not consistent in adopting such apparent choices." He cites the final line of "He preached upon 'Breadth' till it argued him narrow" (V1207), which in the fair copy reads "To meet so enabled a Man" even though on the earlier draft her underlined suggestion was "so *Religious* a man."[43] Among others, poems numbered V1209, V1211, and V1232 could be added to this example. Emily Dickinson was arbitrary and inconsistent in selecting from her own alternates, and that, to quote Mr. Johnson again, makes "clear that no pattern applicable to a 'final' text of unfinished drafts can ever be established."[44]

Thus with no authorial preference and no discernible pattern to apply to semifinal drafts, they must remain unfinished. If we want the poems in a finished state, we must apply other principles of selection and must take the responsibility for doing so. All of the poems mentioned on page 130 are semifinal drafts that were redacted into fair copies by the early editors and included in the first edition of 1890. Some thirty-five poems in that volume—almost a third—were arranged for publication in this way. If we were to abide strictly by the basic principle of editing, those poems would remain unfinished, printed only in a variorum text. A readers' edition based on that principle is impossible. Now that Emily Dickinson has gained the fame that belongs to her, a variorum has been commercially possible, but the editors of 1890 did not have this advantage, and one form of each poem was a publishing necessity. Since they were editing a readers' edition, it was even desirable. Today while hailing the variorum as a great achievement, critics have called for a readers' edition also.[45] Since under Mr. Johnson's hand the poems have reverted to the state in which they were in the 1880's, to have such an edition demands doing afresh the job that Mrs. Todd and Colonel Higginson did then.

As Mr. Johnson suggested to the English Institute, even fair copies may not carry Emily Dickinson's final intention for a

poem. The poem numbered V1437—"A Dew sufficed itself"—
exists in a semifinal draft and four fair copies. In 1874 the poet,
choosing alternate readings, produced a "variant" fair copy from
the semifinal draft, and in the same year she made fair copy II,
whose three extant stanzas read the same as the corresponding
stanzas in fair copy I. Then in 1878 she made two other fair
copies; the first differed from each of its predecessors, but the
second had the same text as the semifinal draft.[46] Mr. Johnson
suggested that from this "one may infer that intermediary texts
even in fair copies had no finality so long as she was attempting
to establish a reading."[47] If, in this example, the poem were extant only up to fair copy III, one might conclude that to be her
final intention. Mr. Johnson concluded fair copy IV to be,[48] but
should another fair copy be found—and there are manuscripts
still missing—even fair copy IV could lose authority. But the
problem affects more than simply these four fair copies. Since
Emily Dickinson did not publish, we do not know when fair
copies are "intermediary," for we have no terminus. Had she
published, she would have committed herself to a finality. And
without that terminus how are we to say what is intermediary and
what is final in any fair copy?[49]

Moreover, Mr. Johnson assumes that there was a unity in
Emily Dickinson's intent, that she was trying to establish *a*
reading. Multiplicity, however, did not bother this poet, and she
would without qualms change a reading in order to make it
appropriate for different people and different occasions. Each of
these fair copies is "final" for its person or occasion, but that
cannot be equated with final intention for publication. Sending
a poem to a friend is a type of publishing, but it fixes the poem
only for that person on that occasion; sending a poem to a
publisher is distinctly different and, in theory, fixes the form of
the poem for all people and all time. Had Emily Dickinson prepared the above poem for publication, she easily could have
chosen fair copy II or III in preference to IV. Thus because they
lack a terminus and because they have an occasional nature, fair
copies are not reliable as an indication of final intention for
publication.

We lack, then, authorial final intention throughout the poems of Emily Dickinson. If we were to read the poems as she wrote them and as she intended them, we could not progress beyond a full variorum edition, or more strictly, not beyond the manuscripts. To get beyond this state, we must face the compromises forced upon us. Most rough drafts of unfinished poems probably do not belong in any edition except a variorum. As for semifinal drafts, one form of each poem will have to be selected. Poems that exist in a single fair copy should be taken as they are, but from the variant fair copies of a single poem we should choose its best.[50]

Mr. Johnson approached the textual problems again in 1960 when he published the one-volume edition, *The Complete Poems of Emily Dickinson*. He excluded from this edition all the notes to the poems and printed only one version of each poem, yet tried to avoid conscious decision in doing so. From variant fair copies he usually printed the earliest, since that was usually the principal representation in the variorum; better versions were at times eliminated with the notes.[51] There were occasions when he did not choose: when he printed two versions of "Safe in their Alabaster Chambers" (V216) and when in the introduction he listed the fair copy variants of "Blazing in Gold and quenching in Purple" (V228) and said, "The reader may make the choice."[52]

Concerning semifinal and rough drafts, the editor should speak for himself:

> Selection becomes mandatory for the semifinal drafts. Though by far the largest number of packet copies exist in but a single fair-copy version, several exist in semifinal form: those for which marginally the poet suggested an alternate reading for one word or more. In order to keep editorial construction to a bare minimum, I have followed the policy of adopting such suggestions only when they are underlined, presumably Emily Dickinson's method of indicating her own preference.
>
> Rough drafts, of which there are relatively few, are allowed to stand as such, with no editorial tinkering.[53]

In his readers' edition, Mr. Johnson faced the same problems with which any editor of such an edition must cope, and these problems led him into contradictions with the findings of the variorum. The poems that exist in semifinal form amount, by his tally in 1955, to "some three hundred."[54] That he here claims to follow a policy for them is inconsistent with his variorum statement that "no pattern applicable to a 'final' text of unfinished drafts can ever be established. Semifinal drafts, unless she herself redacted them into fair copies, must always remain unfinished."[55] A policy, any policy, followed in regard to alternates is tantamount to making a decision—here, a decision by default. Then too, as demonstrated in the variorum,[56] the acceptance of underlined words cannot be established as a consistent pattern of choice by the poet and therefore not for the editor. Finally, most rough drafts are mere unfinished sketches of poems, of which in this edition we get only part of the fragment. Of what value is a worksheet without all the work? It is doubtful that an adequate "complete" edition of Emily Dickinson's poems can exist outside the variorum.

I have selected a few familiar poems from the edition of 1890 for comparison with their text in Mr. Johnson's 1960 edition. Mr. Johnson follows the arbitrary pattern of choosing marginal suggestions in semifinal drafts only when they are underlined. The early editors, it should be remembered, made the choices for the first edition critically. Mr. Johnson is thus either undoing or confirming their work. Using the variorum text for the poems and alternate readings, I will first refer to two poems that are improved in the 1960 edition and then to two that are not.

> The Soul selects her own Society— (V303)
> Then—shuts the Door—
> To her divine Majority—
> Present no more—

> 3. To] On
> 4. Present] Obtrude

. . . .

> I'm Nobody! Who are you?   (V288)
> Are you—Nobody—too?
> Then there's a pair of us!
> Dont tell! they'd banish us—you know!

>   4. banish us⟧ *advertise*

In spite of the loss both of assonance and the flavor of the word
"obtrude," the first poem is improved by the rejection of the
alternates. The shut door protecting the select society is im-
penetrable. Others cannot obtrude; they can only present themselves, which is exactly what the emperor does in the second
stanza of this poem. It is even impossible to obtrude upon the
soul's attention, for she remains unmoved by the emperor; indeed she closes "the Valves of her attention— / Like Stone." In
the second poem quoted above, Mr. Johnson printed "advertise"
in the 1960 edition since the word was underlined. Here again
the 1960 version is more appropriate to the sense: to a nobody
who wants to remain a nobody, being advertised is a worse fate
than being banished.

The following are two selections that are not improved in the
1960 edition.

> If certain, when this life was out—   (V511)
> That your's and mine, should be—
> I'd toss it yonder, like a Rind,
> And take Eternity—

>   (16) 4. take⟧ taste

.   .   .   .

> I asked no other thing—   (V621)
> No other—was denied—
> I offered Being—for it—
> The Mighty Merchant sneered—

> Brazil? He twirled a Button—
> Without a glance my way—
> "But—Madam—is there nothing else—
> That We can show—Today?"

>   4. sneered⟧ smiled—

The early editors accepted both suggestions for the poems; the 1960 edition eliminated both. In the first example (fourth stanza of "If you were coming in the Fall"), the alternate reading completes a metaphor where "taste" links with "Rind": under the condition of certainty the speaker would throw away the rind (life) and taste the inner fruit (eternity with him). In the second poem the better word is the alternate "smiled." "Sneered," for all its onomatopoetic qualities, is too strong. It destroys the patronizing tone of the Merchant and overshadows the reductio comparison in the next line between "Brazil?" and "Button." Moreover, "smiled" in this context includes a sneer and in a much subtler way.

If Mr. Johnson had printed the famous poem "I taste a liquor never brewed" (V214) according to the policy he set forth in his introduction to the 1960 volume, the first and last stanzas would have appeared this way:

> I taste a liquor never brewed—
> From Tankards scooped in Pearl—
> Not all the Frankfort Berries
> Yield such an Alcohol!

and

> Till Seraphs swing their snowy Hats—
> And Saints—to windows run—
> To see the little Tippler   15
> From Manzanilla come!

The familiar alternate suggestions for the third line and the last were adopted, however, even though they were not underlined:

> 3. Frankfort Berries] Vats upon the Rhine
> 16. From Manzanilla come!] Leaning against the—Sun—

Similarly, from the alternates to another famous poem, "I like to see it lap the Miles" (V585)—

> 1. see it] hear it—
> 9. sides] Ribs—
> 14. And] And, or then—
> 15. prompter than] punctual as—

Mr. Johnson adopted the alternate suggestions for lines 9 and 15, although once again they were not underlined. Evidently he found that an arbitrary policy did not do justice to the poems. His selections in these two instances can be justified only by invoking critical judgment.[57]

CRITICISM AND EDITING

Something remains to be said about approaches to poetry, specifically as they relate to Emily Dickinson's textual problems. The biographical approach, one of the oldest modes of literary study, can be illustrated by quoting from John Ciardi's review of the variorum edition and Mr. Johnson's biography of the poet:

> For what Johnson centrally attests is what every well-engaged reader knows—that the biography of a poet is his poems, once we have learned to read them.
>
> . . . every poet of consequence writes his life into the Grand Poem which is the total of his individual poems . . . .
>
> It is now possible for the first time to read Emily Dickinson's poems as she wrote them, as she lived with them and into them, and as she meant them to be read.[58]

If one attempts to approach the poet through her works, one must have those works as she left them. Not only unaltered but unedited texts would be necessary, since, as we have seen, any editorial work is a construction upon the poems. The biographical critic, as editor, can never go beyond the manuscripts or a complete literal rendering of them. It is only by a compromise of his principle—that there is something approximating a one-to-one correspondence between an author's life and his work—that we can have the poems in a readers' edition.

The biographical approach goes at the poet through his poems; another mode of literary study approaches the poems through the poet. Robert Hillyer spoke for this approach when he said in a review that the variorum edition "restores to us, unaltered, her full poetical achievement."[59] If we are attempting to determine the full poetical achievement of a poet, we must demand unaltered texts, that is, only the work of the poet. To assess Emily Dickinson's full poetical achievement would require not only unchanged texts, but unedited texts as well, since her full poetical achievement is limited to her manuscripts. On this basis it becomes practically impossible to make comment upon a poem which exists in a semifinal draft, for all the possibilities would have to be considered simultaneously *in toto.* We in our discussion could not choose among the alternates, for the poet herself did not. Almost all that could be said critically about poems in semifinal drafts is that they are unfinished. Critically, this is equivalent to what Mr. Johnson said editorially about them: "Semifinal drafts, unless she herself redacted them into fair copies, must always remain unfinished."[60]

Critically or editorially, it is the same stumbling block of authorial intention. Editorially, with few exceptions, authorial final intention has been the basic principle followed. The results have sometimes disappointed. Ronald B. McKerrow, attempting to publish Nashe's final intention for *The Unfortunate Traveller,* of which there were two authorized editions, printed the second edition even though some of the new readings were "manifestly inferior to those of the first."[61] André Morize suggested that sometimes it might be better to print earlier versions and received a rebuke from Chauncey Sanders for his boldness.[62] Yet Morize's suggestion is sometimes followed. Malcolm Cowley justified his reprinting the 1855 edition of *Leaves of Grass* by claiming that that edition contained Whitman's "freshest and boldest style" and that "later corrections were also corruptions of the style and concealments of the original meaning."[63] The complaint is that the classic editorial principle can do injustice to the work as art.

The contemporary critical climate rules that we consider the poems as poems, and here the difficult problem arises: just what *is* the relationship between an author and his work? Critically, we say that a work of art is not commensurate with its author's intentions, yet the basic text is recovered, edited, and printed on the basis of authorial intention (so that the critic can then go to work with the theory that it is not commensurate with those intentions). It is an anomaly within our discipline and one that is not always recognized. "That this has become an age of criticism is a commonplace," write William M. Gibson and Edwin H. Cady. "But," they continue, "that the very fact of our critical concern has also produced in the United States a generation of sensitive and, for historical and technical reasons, uniquely competent editors of literary texts is far less generally known."[64] The conflicting bases of criticism and editing must be even less generally known if our critical concern has been the effective cause for the rise of a generation of editors. Why should a critic call for a "clear" text—one based on the author's intentions—when critically he disallows those intentions? The state of the Dickinson manuscripts could force us to be consistent, even to an extreme, in our critical principles since we lack the other standard.

Thus in the critical work of Charles R. Anderson, who, recognizing that there is no authorial final intention for Emily Dickinson's poems, has chosen freely among her alternate suggestions in constructing his texts, we have Mr. Anderson's exegesis helping to establish the text of the poem upon which that exegesis itself is based. The validity of both poem and criticism would appear questionable. But a literary work of art, it can be argued, has a peculiar mode of existence. Although Emily Dickinson may have considered her semifinal drafts as the drafts of a single poem, multiplicity did not bother her, and she herself would copy them out in different ways, each of which can be considered a different poem. In the strictest sense we have as many poems as we have combinations of alternates. At the present time there are at least four such poems published about Miss Dickinson's famous locomotive.[65] They usually begin "I like to see it lap the Miles" (V585). Because he chose a different reading, the first two stanzas in Mr. Anderson's book read as follows:

> I like to hear it lap the Miles—
> And lick the Valleys up—
> And stop to feed itself at Tanks—
> And then—prodigious step
>
> Around a Pile of Mountains—
> And supercilious peer
> In Shanties—by the sides of Roads—
> And then a Quarry pare[66]

Mr. Anderson's explanation that Emily Dickinson "staged a private celebration in her mind" is supported by the verb "hear" in the first line. The relationship of the *persona* to the materials of the poem is quite different from that in "I like to see it lap the Miles." In the latter all is externalized, but in the above poem the events are truly a mental celebration. Although Mr. Anderson would perhaps be more critically consistent in ascribing this to the *persona* and not to Emily Dickinson, his criticism is perfectly valid for the above poem if it is considered a poem itself and not a version of another poem.

Using the poem as a standard unto itself, one might even argue that corrupt texts are legitimate. We know that Mrs. Todd altered the second stanza of "These are the days when Birds come back" (V130) to read:

> These are the days when skies put on
> The old, old sophistries of June,—
> A blue and gold mistake.[67]

"Put on" in the first line was Mrs. Todd's emendation, and it fits quite well here, for it means "put on" both in the sense to dress and to feign. With the original reading, "skies resume," the meaning of the stanza and of the poem is different, particularly in its attitude toward nature. If Indian summer is a resumption of the sophistries of June, then the question of man's relationship to nature is answered by the assertion that all of nature, not just Indian summer, is a deceptively colored mistake. If one follows the principles that form and meaning are inseparable in a literary work of art and that it is an organic whole, a totality encompassing and dependent upon all its parts, then one would have to conclude that even in this unauthorized case each is a different poem with a different existence, history, form and meaning, and that criticism that sticks to the poem itself is valid.

Allen Tate called "Because I could not stop for Death" (V712) one of "the perfect poems in English" and declared that "if the word great means anything in poetry, this poem is one of the greatest in the English language."[68] Yet in the text he was using there was a full stanza missing and editorial alterations in four lines.[69] George F. Whicher similarly appraised "Success is counted sweetest" (V67), saying that it was organically perfect and that no word could be changed, added, or deleted.[70] Yet "break" in the final line had been an editorial substitution for "burst."[71] Most critics caught with their text showing in such a manner would probably feel embarrassment and issue a call for a "clear" text. Yet is there a defense for Mr. Tate's and Mr. Whicher's comments? A poem, one might argue, is a poem is a poem. Clearly, even an altered poem *is*. And within the context of poetry in general, criticism of such a poem is perfectly valid. The error, the deception, comes in passing off these poems as Emily Dickinson's. They are Dickinson-Todd-Higginson's. They are, quite simply, poetry.

But we are not commonly organized in our pursuit of literature to talk about literature *per se*. Fortunately or unfortunately, authors are our categories, and there is little space for hybrid poems. We have no such category as Dickinson-Todd-Higginson, and the fact that we are not organized to talk about an altered poem as a poem shows how little the subject of our pursuit is poetry. There are, as Emerson might have said, two laws discrete, not reconciled, law for poet and law for poem—law for editor and law for critic. Just as Emerson insisted upon seeing Platonically (or neo-Platonically) and was disturbed when his generation pursued an Aristotelian path to materialism, so there is a disturbing conflict in our discipline between what might be called a Platonic approach to editing and an Aristotelian approach to criticism. Plato conceived each Idea as eternal, unchanging, complete, and perfect in its own way, whereas each appearance was temporal, changing, incomplete, and imperfect even in its own way. Similarly, in editing, the author's final intention is like a Platonic archetype, unchanging, complete, and perfect in its own way, against which any one of its appearances in print can be corrected. Unfortunately, an author's intentions are not necessarily eternal and may exist as precariously as do any of their appearances: destroying a manuscript may destroy all trace of intention. Moreover, the separate appearances, even as an altered poem, have an existence as real as the archetype. Aristotle saw pure form without matter as mere abstraction, matter without form as simple potentiality. Matter and form together constitute the particular—reality itself. So, too, the union of form and content constitutes the particular poem, upon which the critic exercises his interest without reference to the archetypal intentions of an author.

Academically raised in an era that believes in the sacredness of the author's text and that also believes in criticism divorced from authorial intention, we face a quandary with the Dickinson texts. The principle of editing that a text exactly represent the author's final intention is inadequate, since finality cannot be established. Actually any approach that is exclusively author-oriented will fail editorially. If one attempts, with a biographical concern, to approach the poet through her works, one must have those works exactly as she left them. Likewise, if we are attempting to evaluate the achievement of a poet, we need only the poet's work.

If, then, we want the poems in a readers' edition, we are forced to make decisions. But this, too, can lead to the impossible. "Those fair—fictitious People" (V499) exists in a semi-final draft with twenty-six suggestions that fit eleven places in the poem. From this, 7680 poems are possible—not versions but, according to our critical principles, poems.[72] To consider each would be the editorial work of a lifetime. Yet to be totally faithful to our critical position, such would be demanded.

What is needed in order to have a readers' edition is the development and demonstration of a new editorial procedure for material unprepared by the author for publication. This would necessitate a compromise between the demands of authorial intention and the demands of the poems. Poems are neither self-generating nor self-maturing, and those which lack completion by Emily Dickinson will have to be finished by an editor. That editor, in trying to avoid the twin pitfalls of arbitrariness and relativism, in trying to reconcile the conflict within our discipline, will have to struggle with editorial and critical principles even to the limits of ontology and epistemology. He will be editor, critic, and philosopher in one.

Reference Matter

Notes

CHAPTER I

1   Mabel Loomis Todd, diary, January 18, 1891, quoted in Millicent Todd Bingham, *Ancestors' Brocades: The Literary Debut of Emily Dickinson* (New York: Harper, 1945), p. 106n.

2   *Ancestors' Brocades,* p. 138.

3   Lavinia Dickinson to Mrs. C. S. Mack, February 17, 1891, quoted in Thomas H. Johnson, ed., *The Poems of Emily Dickinson,* 3 vols. (Cambridge: Harvard University Press, 1955), I, xxxixn. This edition will hereafter be cited as the variorum or as *Poems* (1955), and my references to Emily Dickinson's poems will use its numbering prefixed by a *V*. The later printings of the variorum (1958, 1963) list some errata.

4   Lavinia Dickinson called these gatherings "volumes"; Mrs. Todd called them "volumes" or "fascicules." Millicent Todd Bingham used "fascicle," and for a long time it was the common term. More recently the variorum introduced the word "packet," and it has gained currency. In this study "volume," "fascicle," and "packet" will be used synonymously when referring to Emily Dickinson's bound gatherings of poems.

5   *Ancestors' Brocades,* p. 18.

6   M. L. Todd quoted in *Ancestors' Brocades,* p. 2.

7   M. L. Todd, journal, September 12, 1881, quoted in Jay Leyda, *The Years and Hours of Emily Dickinson,* 2 vols. (New Haven: Yale University Press, 1960), II, 352.

8   M. L. Todd. "Emily Dickinson's Literary Début," *Harper's Magazine,* CLX (March 1930), 463.

9   Todd, diary, May 15, 1886, quoted in *Ancestors' Brocades,* p. 13.
10 Todd, *Harper's,* CLX, 464.
11 *Ibid.*
12 M. L. Todd, unpublished journal, February 2, 1886.
13 M. L. Todd quoted in Millicent Todd Bingham, *Mabel Loomis Todd: Her Contributions to the Town of Amherst* (New York: privately printed, 1935), p. 3.
14 *Ancestors' Brocades,* p. 20. The variorum (I, xl) erroneously dates this trip March to November.
15 M. L. Todd, unpublished diary, November 30, 1887. The italics are mine.

In 1898 Mrs. Todd testified that she had begun "to copy a few of the poems early in the summer of 1886, when Emily Dickinson had been dead about a month or six weeks" (Superior Court of Hampshire County, Massachusetts, 1898, docket no. 125). Her testimony, however, came over ten years after the fact, and she was probably mistaken about the schedule. Her diary for 1886 does not mention any copying that summer; in fact she was away from Amherst, traveling, during much of the vacation. Copying is first mentioned in February 1887: on the thirteenth Mrs. Todd "went to Vinnie's, & she read me a few more *scraps* of Emily's" (my italics). On the seventeenth she copied "a few of Emily's poems . . . on the typewriter," and on the following day she "went over to Vinnie's with some copied poems."

Clearly, a few poems had been transcribed before Mrs. Todd's trip to Japan (June–October 1887). But, apart from the brief mention in February 1887, there is no record in the diaries of copying until after the return from Japan. One should note that the poems Mrs. Todd did copy in February 1887 were apparently "scraps"—that is, poems on loose, odd-shaped scraps of paper—not the poems in the fascicles. And this is in accord with Lavinia's letter of December 23, 1890 (*Ancestors' Brocades,* p. 87), and with Mrs. Todd's statement in her journal (*Ancestors' Brocades,* p. 401) that after Emily Dickinson's death the manuscripts (that is, the fascicles) had been in Susan Dickinson's possession for nearly two years before Mrs. Todd herself received them. In this study I date the beginning of the copying as November 1887, though Mrs. Todd had certainly transcribed a few poems, apparently scraps, before then.

16 Anna Mary Wells, *Dear Preceptor: The Life and Times of Thomas Wentworth Higginson* (Boston: Houghton Mifflin, 1963), pp. 276–77.

17 For example, the unpublished diary entries for January 22, February 15, March 11, April 16, 17, and May 8, 1888.

18 M. L. Todd, journal, November 30, 1890, quoted in *Ancestors' Brocades,* p. 402. Mrs. Todd's husband may have typed copies of a few of the poems, but since his copies—if any survive—cannot be distinguished from Mrs. Todd's, I will refer to all the typescripts as hers.

19 The surviving transcripts are now in the Emily Dickinson Collection of the Amherst College Library (cited hereafter as the Amherst Collection). The two typescripts mentioned here are in the Amherst Collection, Box 28, 1896 printer's copy, pp. 79, 69.

20 It is not clear whether the purple ribbon or the black ribbon came first, but both were used during the first part of the first year of copying.

21 The World typewriter is now in the Jones Library, Amherst, Massachusetts.

22 *Poems* (1955), I, xli.

23 Identification of small snatches of handwriting is a difficult job at best; when they are only numbers, it is even harder. The numbering of the packets, mostly in blue pencil, appears to me to have been largely done by Mrs. Todd. Millicent Todd Bingham, who is thoroughly familiar with her mother's handwriting, agrees.

24 The discussion here and in the remainder of the chapter is based on the variorum arrangement and numbering of the packets. Chapter II of this study proposes a different arrangement.

25 Todd, journal, November 30, 1890, quoted in *Ancestors' Brocades,* p. 402.

26 *Ibid.*

27 An Amherst spinster, aged 28, later Mrs. Charles M. Houghton.

28 Todd, unpublished diary for 1889.

29 Amherst Collection, Box 28, 1896 printer's copy, p. 139.

30 Todd, journal, November 30, 1890, quoted in *Ancestors' Brocades,* p. 402.

31 *Ibid.,* p. 403.

32 Amherst Collection, Box 1, packet 90, leaf 13.

33 Amherst Collection, Box 28, 1896 printer's copy, p. 43.

34 The variorum, however, also transcribes this final dash as a period.

35 This description applies only to first copies of poems. Second or later copies frequently incorporated changes that are not so easily discerned. It is usually possible, however, to determine a first from a second or later copy by comparing the copies with

the transcript pattern of the packet containing the poem (see Ch. III).

The transcript patterns have an even larger potential. They can greatly aid an editor in judging whether a transcript that agrees with no extant manuscript actually represents a variant version that has been lost or whether it merely contains a scribal error. For example, the transcript for "Trudging to Eden" (V1020) differs in the last line from the only surviving manuscript of the poem. That line in transcript reads "New acquaintance, this boy made"; the manuscript in packet 90 reads "New Acquaintance—this Baby made." Was there another (variant) manuscript or is the transcript in error? A full study of the transcripts for this packet shows that the poems in it were handcopied by Mrs. Todd onto paper X and X-2 and that "Trudging to Eden" would have been copied onto X-2. The variant transcript is the only transcript extant for the poem, and since it is on paper X-2, an editor could conclude with confidence that the transcript was made from packet 90. The difference in readings, therefore, should be attributed to Mrs. Todd as a scribal error.

36 T. W. Higginson to Lavinia Dickinson, April 8, 1890, quoted in *Ancestors' Brocades,* pp. 50–51.

37 Though Mrs. Todd and Colonel Higginson could not have known it, Thomas Niles had tried in 1882 and 1883 to persuade Emily Dickinson to allow Roberts Brothers to publish a volume of her poems; see letters numbered 749b (1882) and 813b (1883) in *The Letters of Emily Dickinson,* ed. Thomas H. Johnson, 3 vols. (Cambridge: Harvard University Press, 1958), III, 726, 769, hereafter cited as *Letters* (1958). See also *Poems* (1955), I, xliv, and Thomas H. Johnson, *Emily Dickinson: An Interpretive Biography* (Cambridge: Harvard University Press, 1955), pp. 175–76.

38 Thomas Niles to T. W. Higginson, June 10, 1890, quoted in *Ancestors' Brocades,* p. 53.

39 Arlo Bates to Thomas Niles, undated, quoted in *Ancestors' Brocades,* p. 52.

40 *Ibid.,* p. 53.

41 Bates to Niles, undated, Amherst Collection, Box 20, To 238: "I have taken the trouble to number the poems, and these are those which I should include: 1–2–4–5–6–7–8–12–15–17–22–23–25[?Does not this belong in the 2nd section, as 'Wedded'] 26–27–31–32–33[I do not like the name suggested.]36–37–38–44–46–47–48–50–51–52–53–55–58–59–61–62–64–68–69–70–

71–72–76–78–79–80–81–82–84–85–87–88–89–91–93–98–99–
101–105–106 109–110–112[for a single line!]–114–[Of 115
the figure is used better elsewhere in the volume.]–116–120–
123–127[should be 'Death' in sec. 4th.]–133b–135[for the last
stanza.]–138–140–141–145–149–150–151–154–156–157–160–
161–163–165–166–167–169–170–171–172–174–175–[Oh, the
wickedness of the difference between the exquisite beginning
and the awkward ending!]–182–186–194–195–197–198–199
[the proposed title seems to me exactly wrong.]–201–202[but
it is so inferior to the one preceding it that it would not do to
end with.]"

42 *Ancestors' Brocades,* p. 53.

43 The transcripts marked by Bates for rejection are scattered in
the Amherst Collection through Boxes 19, 28, 29–1, and 29–2.
His surviving numbers are here given with the variorum num-
bers of the poems: 11 (V540), 18 (V609), 28 (V117), 34
(V85), 41 (V212), 45 (V453), 49 (V537), 54 (V725), 57
(V246), 60 (V271), 63 (V909), 65 (V616—final two
stanzas), 67 (V63), 75 (V176), 86 (V591), 92 (V419), 94
(V1079), 95 (V1593), 104 (V1115), 117 (V235), 118
(V1034), 121 (V386), 122 (V300), 124 (V507), 125
(V1114), 126 (V798), 128 (V100), 129 (V554), 130
(V129), 132 (V827), 133 (V734), 142 (V279), 143 (V145),
164 (V463), 167 (V521), 173 (V80), 176 (V261), 178
(V964), 181 (V425), 185 (V382), 187 (V104), 189 (V410),
190 (V96), 193 (V68). It will be noted that 167 appears here
and on the list of recommendations (see n. 41 above); what
happened is that Arlo Bates recommended 167 (V521) for
publication, but the editors withdrew it anyway. Three other
poems can be placed among those rejected by Bates. Each transcript has his X on it, but the number on each has been either
erased or destroyed. The three poems are V726 and V908 in the
Amherst Collection, Box 28, 1896 printer's copy, pp. 161 and
127, and V122 in Box 29–2. Finally, another five of Bates' re-
jections, which the editors published over his objections, are
named in the next paragraph in the text of this study: V449,
V216, V324, V187, and V193.

44 *Ancestors' Brocades,* pp. 54–55, 404.

45 T. W. Higginson to M. L. Todd, July 3, 6, 1890, quoted in
Ancestors' Brocades, p. 55.

46 *Poems* (1955), I, xliii–xlvii.

47 T. W. Higginson, quoted in *Ancestors' Brocades,* p. 58.

48 *Ancestors' Brocades,* p. 58; Todd, *Harper's,* CLX, 467.

49 *Ancestors' Brocades,* pp. 41–43; and Higginson to Todd, January 5, 1891, Amherst Collection, Box 20, To 23.

50 *Poems* (1955), I, xlv.

51 Bates to Niles, undated, quoted in *Ancestors' Brocades,* p. 53.

52 Todd, journal, November 30, 1890, quoted in *Ancestors' Brocades,* p. 403.

53 *Ancestors' Brocades,* p. 54.

54 Wells, *Dear Preceptor,* pp. 278–79. Mrs. Wells misquotes Higginson here, the exact quotation being "in her—so to speak—unregenerate condition."

55 T. W. Higginson, "Emily Dickinson's Letters," *Atlantic Monthly,* LXVIII (October 1891), 448.

56 Higginson to Todd, June 11, 1890, quoted in *Ancestors' Brocades,* p. 54.

57 Higginson to Todd, July 14, 1890, quoted in *Ancestors' Brocades,* p. 56.

58 Unpublished letter from Higginson to Todd, undated, Amherst Collection, Box 20, To 15.

59 Higginson to Todd, August 26, 1890, quoted in *Ancestors' Brocades,* p. 62.

60 T. W. Higginson, "Preface," in *Poems by Emily Dickinson,* ed. Mabel Loomis Todd and T. W. Higginson (Boston: Roberts Brothers, 1890), p. v.

61 As, for example, in "There's a certain Slant of light" (V258) and "To know just how He suffered—would be dear" (V622).

62 In lines 6 and 8 of "If you were coming in the Fall" (V511).

63 In line 7 of "The Soul selects her own Society" (V303).

64 Line 10 of "Glee—The great storm is over" (V619).

65 It is not possible to say precisely how many of each kind of change were made by the editors, for without the printer's copy for the first series, which, like the printer's copy for the second series, has been destroyed, one cannot be fully sure what is an alteration, a printer's error, or a misreading of the manuscripts. The printer's copy for the third series, edited by Mrs. Todd alone, survives in the Amherst College Library. For a note on the editorial changes in the third series, see below, Ch. III, n. 16.

66 T. W. Higginson, "An Open Portfolio," *Christian Union,* XLII (September 25, 1890), 392–93.

67 Lilian Whiting, "Poems," *Boston Budget,* November 23, 1890.

68 Arlo Bates, "Miss Dickinson's Poems," *Boston Courier,* November 23, 1890.

69 Louise Chandler Moulton, "A Very Remarkable Book," *Boston Sunday Herald,* November 23, 1890.

70   William Dean Howells, "Editor's Study," *Harper's Magazine,*
     LXXXII (January 1891), 320.
71   "The Newest Poet," *Daily News* (London), January 2, 1891.
72   Thomas Bailey Aldrich, "*In Re* Emily Dickinson," *Atlantic
     Monthly,* LXIX (January 1892), 144.
73   *Ancestors' Brocades,* p. 109n.
74   Amherst Collection, Box 20, To 313, contains lists of both
     Mrs. Todd's and Lavinia's selections.
75   Todd to Higginson, July 13, 1891, quoted in *Ancestors' Bro-
     cades,* p. 137. Mrs. Todd's list of the "Contents of Volume II
     as sent to Col. Higginson July 13, 1891" is in the Amherst
     Collection, Box 20, To 313.
76   Higginson to Todd, April 21, 1891, quoted in *Ancestors'
     Brocades,* p. 127.
77   Todd to Higginson, July 13, 1891, quoted in *Ancestors' Bro-
     cades,* p. 137.
78   Wells, *Dear Preceptor,* pp. 287–88.
79   Higginson to Todd, July 18, 1891, quoted in *Ancestors' Bro-
     cades,* p. 141.
80   Todd to Higginson, July 22, 1891, quoted in *Ancestors' Bro-
     cades,* p. 144.
81   Todd to Higginson, August 23, 1891, quoted in *Ancestors'
     Brocades,* p. 160.
82   Higginson to Todd, August 26, 1891, quoted in *Ancestors'
     Brocades,* p. 161.
83   Todd to Higginson, September 10, 1891, quoted in *Ancestors'
     Brocades,* p. 162.

CHAPTER II

1   Mabel Loomis Todd, journal, September 20, 1891, quoted in
     Millicent Todd Bingham, *Ancestors' Brocades: The Literary
     Debut of Emily Dickinson* (New York: Harper, 1945), p. 134.
2   M. L. Todd, diary, July 18, 1891, quoted in *Ancestors' Bro-
     cades,* p. 141n.
3   Now in the Amherst Collection, Box 19.
4   See, however, the discussion of "Going to Him! Happy letter!"
     (V494) in n. 51, below, and the discussion of packet 80 in the
     text of this chapter.
5   *Poems* (1955), I, xl–xli.
6   It should be pointed out that the numbering of envelopes may
     have extended beyond 110. If it did, it is not especially sig-
     nificant at present, since all the loose poems have been removed
     from the envelopes and arranged alphabetically in the Amherst

Collection. More recently the envelopes themselves have gone to the Yale University Library.

7 Amherst Collection, Box 1.

8 Cf. below, n. 40.

9 This description of the manuscripts is based on the current arrangement at the Amherst College Library and at the Houghton Library. This chapter will propose a revised order for the threaded packets listed here.

10 *Poems* (1955), I, xli.

11 *Ibid.*

12 *Ibid.*, I, xlii.

13 *Ibid.*, III, 1203–5.

14 M. L. Todd quoted in *Ancestors' Brocades,* p. 17.

15 *Ibid.*

16 M. L. Todd, "Emily Dickinson's Literary Début," *Harper's Magazine,* CLX (March 1930), 464.

17 Todd, journal, November 30, 1890, quoted in *Ancestors' Brocades,* pp. 402, 403; Lavinia Dickinson to Mrs. C. S. Mack, February 17, 1891, quoted in *Poems* (1955), I, xxxix*n.*

18 Appendix 5 of the variorum (III, 1202) strangely dates packet 10, which has only one poem, as 1858 "in part."

19 *Poems* (1955), I, xlii.

20 Occasionally there were extra numbers, as in H 54A. The loose sheets at Houghton commenced numbering at 220.

21 They are sheet H 11 in packet 3, H 29 in packet 7, H 35 in packet 8, H 63 in packet 13, H 70 in packet 29, H 75 in packet 14, H 126 in packet 23, H 155 in packet 29, H 194 and H 195 in packet 36.

22 H 126 in packet 23, H 155 in packet 29, and H 194 in packet 36.

23 H 11 in packet 3, H 29 in packet 7, H 35 in packet 8, H 63 in packet 13, H 75 in packet 14, and H 195 in packet 36.

24 Amherst Collection, Box 20, To 313.

25 Amherst Collection, Box 29–1. Miss Graves copied the first stanza on the first page of the transcript and the rest of the poem on the second page. By July–August 1891 the two parts of the transcript had become separated, and Mrs. Todd classed the second page as a *C* and entered it in the notebook as "When thrones accost my hands." When she went through the packets recording their numbers in the notebook, she of course found no poem in the packets with this as the first line; consequently she recorded no number next to the entry in the notebook. There is, however, a *14* next to the entry. This number is so

unlike the others in the book that I doubt it is Mrs. Todd's, but even if it should prove to be hers, the argument in the text of this chapter is not altered.

26 Amherst Collection, Box 29–1.

27 Amherst Collection, Box 20, To 313.

28 Amherst Collection, Box 19, Tr 2a.

29 *Poems* (1955), I, xlii–xliii and 342–43.

30 *Ibid.,* I, 343.

31 This transcript is now in the Amherst Collection, Box 29–1, as are the other transcripts discussed in this section.

32 See the canceled entry for "Therefore we do life's labor" on p. 150 of the notebook (Amherst Collection, Box 19).

33 *Further Poems of Emily Dickinson,* ed. Martha Dickinson Bianchi and Alfred Leete Hampson (Boston: Little, Brown, 1929), p. 36.

34 *Poems* (1955), I, xliii.

35 The variorum editor consistently fails to distinguish Miss Graves' writing from Mrs. Todd's, and in *Poems* (1955), III, 1156, he attributes this transcript to Mrs. Todd. It is without doubt Miss Graves'.

36 Mrs. Todd also made a transcript of "A Pit," in which the final line is variant: "Who'se doom—to them?" One cannot tell whether this is Emily Dickinson's variant or whether it is merely a copying error. But the Graves transcript, we may be sure, came from packet 29, for which she was the copyist, and her transcript version best fits with H 157, which is also there.

37 The year in which Emily Dickinson copied a poem into a packet may or may not, of course, be the year in which she wrote the poem; see *Poems* (1955), I, xvii–xx.

38 *Poems* (1955), III, 1209. "My country need not change her gown" was published in 1891 and is therefore on Mrs. Todd's list of the contents of the second series (Amherst Collection, Box 20, To 313). Next to the entry Mrs. Todd has written "Norcross" and "I have too"—indicating that the published version came from the Norcross cousins and that she also had access to a copy in her own possession. No packet number is given for this latter. The variorum does not note that a copy of this poem was sent to the Norcross cousins. It is possible that their copy was not used for the second series since the transcript for the copy in Mrs. Todd's possession is not extant—perhaps because it was used as printer's copy in the second series and then destroyed.

39   If these poems did come from packet 13, then they too can be
      dated as belonging to 1862. It must be emphasized, however,
      that this is only a distant conjecture, for we have no assurance
      that these two poems are the only ones from the first two series
      that might qualify for packet 13. Mr. Johnson lists in Appendix
      11 only poems having no surviving holographs at all. Manu-
      scripts for other poems may also be lost, but if there is at least
      one copy extant, Appendix 11 does not report them as de-
      linquent. Thus there may other poems from the first two series
      which, though not named in this appendix, have a missing
      manuscript that once may have been part of packet 13.

40   The variorum, it should be noted, has dated the Library of Con-
      gress manuscript as belonging to 1873, a year later than the
      date assigned to the rest of packet 36.
           This manuscript had been in Mrs. Todd's exclusive posses-
      sion since at least 1896. The pierced hole in packet 36 (and
      in 33, 35, and 38) was therefore made prior to that date. The
      persons who could have put the brass fasteners in the manu-
      scripts therefore are probably limited to Emily Dickinson,
      Lavinia (or Austin) Dickinson, and Mrs. Todd. It was not
      characteristic of Emily to use a fastener; her method of binding
      was sewing. Mrs. Todd had ten other unthreaded packets (86–
      95) in her possession, yet she did not bind them in any manner.
      One is led to suspect that Lavinia (or Austin) used the brass
      fasteners to bind packets 33, 35, 36, and 38.

41   I am here counting H 54 and H 54A as one.

42   H 130, H 209–213.

43   V827, V902, V903, V904, V905, V906, V907, V908, V909,
      V961, V962, V963, V964, V965, V966, V967, V968, V969,
      V970, V971, V972.

44   *Poems* (1955), I, xlii.

45   *Ibid.,* I, xli.

46   There is also no entry in the notebook for envelope 96, since
      Mrs. Todd did not include the envelope in her inventory. It
      was not in fact numbered 96 until Mrs. Bingham did so in
      the present century. For an explanation of why there is no
      packet 39, see later in the text of this chapter.

47   H 149–50, it should be noted, have two sets of sewing holes.
      The inside set can fit either in packet 5 as Mr. Johnson has
      arranged it or with sheets 151–54 in packet 28. Consequently
      even these other sheets in packet 28 can be made to fit in
      packet 5. The outer set of holes fit neither packet 5 nor 28,
      suggesting that sometime between 1891 and 1950 sheets 149
      and 150 were bound in yet a third position.

48 H 69, H 71, H 72, H 75, H 76, H 77.

49 These three sets of sewing holes are on H 69, H 71–72, and H 75–77. The transcript patterns indicate that each group was copied at a separate time and that, therefore, each was in a separate place.

According to the variorum, there would be three different periods of handwriting since it assigns H 75 and H 76 to 1861 and H 77 to 1862. But these three sheets perhaps belong to the same year, for they appear to be three pieces of a larger sheet of paper that Emily Dickinson tore into sections and then, presumably at a common time, used to copy poems. The appearance of the ink and handwriting, moreover, does not indicate to me that she copied these poems in different years.

50 One must bear in mind that the packet numbering was done many years after Emily Dickinson's death and that it will not always represent her grouping of the manuscripts. If, when the poems are next edited, the fascicles are returned to their original order, I would suggest the present packet numbering be discarded and that the new groupings be labeled differently.

51 Mrs. Todd's list of the contents of the second series (Amherst Collection, Box 20, To 313) suggests that another poem belongs to packet 89: "Going to Him! Happy letter!" (V494). This poem, however, probably does not belong to packet 89, for Emily Dickinson signed the manuscript and folded it in thirds for mailing. Jay Leyda has cataloged it among the poems and letters possibly sent to Samuel Bowles.

52 Amherst Collection, Box 1, Jay Leyda's guide sheet for packet 80.

53 See Amherst Collection, Box 28, 1896 printer's copy, p. 132; Box 29–2; and Box 28, 1896 printer's copy, p. 10, respectively for the transcripts for "Bless God, he went as soldiers" (V147), "If I should cease to bring a Rose" (V56), and "To venerate the simple days" (V57).

54 In 1858, according to the variorum dating.

55 Because this canceled version does not appear in the variorum, the *Concordance to the Poems of Emily Dickinson,* ed. S. P. Rosenbaum (Ithaca: Cornell University Press, 1964) also omits it, and the variant readings, since this concordance is based on the variorum canon. This work will hereafter be cited as *Concordance* (1964).

David J. M. Higgins prints a text of this canceled version and discusses it in his article, "Twenty-five Poems by Emily Dickinson: Unpublished Variant Versions," *American Literature,* XXXVIII (March 1966), 1–21. His printing differs from the manuscript in three ways. The first is the lack of capitalization of "Sister" in line 1. Capitalization is a difficult problem in editing Emily Dickinson's poetry, and frequently one may have trouble determining whether a word should or should not be capitalized, but in this case there should be little doubt that the word begins with a capital: the initial *S* is about twice the size of the second *s*. The other two differences are in stanza 5 ("Violet" for "Violets") and stanza 6 ("whole world's" for "wide night's"). Mr. Higgins suggests that these are authoritative variants, but they are his own misreading of the manuscript or errors in his transcription. The canceled manuscript is not variant in these two places but has exactly the same reading as the version in *Poems* (1955).

Mr. Higgins' text does have authoritative variants in two other places. He accurately indicates that line 1 is variant: it reads "the" instead of "our." Mr. Higgins seems unaware, however, that the fourth line of stanza 5, which he correctly transcribes as "And in her Eye," varies from the corresponding line in the copy sent to Susan Dickinson. There it reads: "Still in her Eye." The canceled manuscript is variant in these two places only.

56   This line (20) is the last on 80–3/8. Emily Dickinson placed an extra long "dash" after it and another before the next line, which is the first on 80–9/4.

57   The variorum editor apparently mistook the scissored edge for the bottom trim edge and therefore believed this uncanceled side was the bottom of the recto of a leaf; *Poems* (1955), I, 43.

58   Amherst Collection, Box 28, 1896 printer's copy, p. 10.

59   *The Complete Poems of Emily Dickinson,* ed. Thomas H. Johnson (Boston: Little, Brown, 1960), p. 30. This edition will hereafter be cited as *Complete Poems* (1960).

60   This was perhaps a printer's error. It was not, however, corrected in the later printings of the variorum, and it was reproduced again in *Complete Poems* (1960). The error has also been carried over into the *Concordance* (1964).

61   Amherst Collection, Box 19, Tr 20.

62   Amherst Collection, Box 28, 1896 printer's copy, p. 70.

63   Upon first coming to Amherst in 1881, Mrs. Todd was a close friend of Susan Dickinson, but about 1883 their friendship ended; see Mrs. Todd's letters, diaries, and journals quoted in Jay Leyda, *The Years and Hours of Emily Dickinson* (New

Haven: Yale University Press, 1960), II, 353, 361, 363, 376, 391, and 396.

64 Millicent Todd Bingham, *Emily Dickinson's Home* (New York: Harper, 1955), pp. 55, 409.

65 M. L. Todd, "Preface," in *Letters of Emily Dickinson* (New York: Harper, 1931), pp. ix–x.

66 Bingham, *Emily Dickinson's Home,* pp. 53–55.

67 The manuscript sheets themselves are not numbered with a 39, yet the transcripts definitely show one. Mrs. Todd therefore must have kept the packets or the transcripts in a numerical order, for a while at least, before she actually wrote the numbers on them in blue pencil.

68 The transcripts with changed location guides are "By such and such an offering," "It did not surprise me," "When I count the seeds," and "If I should cease to bring a Rose" in Amherst Collection, Box 29–2; and "Bless God, he went as soldiers," in Box 28, 1896 printer's copy, p. 132.

69 *Poems* (1955), I, 42, 105.

70 M. L. Todd to T. W. Higginson, October 6, 1891, quoted in *Ancestors' Brocades,* p. 165. The facts in this paragraph come from *Ancestors' Brocades,* pp. 155–71.

71 Arthur Chamberlain, "The Poems of Emily Dickinson," *The Commonwealth* (Boston), December 26, 1891.

72 "Emily Dickinson's Poems," *People and Patriot* (Concord, N.H.), February 1892.

CHAPTER III

1 Millicent Todd Bingham, *Ancestors' Brocades: The Literary Debut of Emily Dickinson* (New York: Harper, 1945), p. 138.

2 "3rd Series" on a transcript can *help* establish that it was one of Mrs. Todd's first copies and therefore generally accurate. Second or later copies often had editorial changes incorporated into them, but such copies were usually made after Mrs. Todd made her selection and therefore will not bear the marking "3rd Series." More transcripts bear this marking than simply the ones used in *Poems* (1896).

3 *Ancestors' Brocades,* p. 201.

4 The marking "Yearbook," like the marking "3rd Series," can aid an editor working with Mrs. Todd's transcripts; see above, n. 2.

5 M. L. Todd, unpublished diary, May 21, 1892.

6 *Ancestors' Brocades,* pp. 201, 204.

7 The editing of *Letters* (1894) is recounted in detail in *Ancestors' Brocades,* pp. 188–323.

8 In the variorum notes to the poems, the editor attempts to give the full publishing history of each poem including any variant readings in the various appearances. In making a survey of the poems in the third series (1896) that had received publication prior to appearing in that volume, I found that these notes are incomplete and at times misleading. For example, V1176 was first published in *Letters* (1894), I, x, not in the third series as the variorum notes indicate. And while the notes correctly name *Letters* (1894) as the first publication of V995, they do not record the next publication of the poem in the third series (1896), naming *Complete Poems* (1924) instead. The editor then speculates that Mrs. Bianchi may have had access to a holograph copy now lost, but the conjecture is unnecessary and misleading: Mrs. Bianchi incorporated the three nineteenth-century editions into *Complete Poems* (1924), and her text of V995 comes from the printing in the third series (1896) that Mr. Johnson does not record. For another example, the variorum does not note the printing of several poems that Mrs. Todd published in the *Bachelor of Arts* (May 1895). V1263 and parts of V93, V149, and V746 were reprinted there, while V1320 and part of V1213 were there published for the first time.

In its account of the publishing history of each poem, the variorum seeks not only to list the various appearances but also to record any variant readings in them. That the variorum has not always succeeded can be seen from a collation of the poems that appeared in magazines before they were collected into the third series (1896). Those that appeared in the *Bachelor of Arts,* some with variant readings, the variorum fails to discover. Another eight have variant readings in their various appearances. Collation shows that the editor has handled four of these correctly but that he has erred on four by not recording these readings (V466, V501, V686, V1732). Such variants are of considerable importance in editing, for each one must be examined to determine whether or not it has any authority.

9 M. L. Todd to E. D. Hardy, December 3, 1894, quoted in *Ancestors' Brocades,* p. 311.

10 *Ibid.*

11 Hardy to Todd, December 11, 1894, quoted in *Ancestors' Brocades,* pp. 311–12.

12 *Ancestors' Brocades,* p. 333.

13 Amherst Collection, Box 28, 1896 printer's copy, pp. 46, 82, 127, and 146 respectively.

14 1896 printer's copy, p. 82.

15 1896 printer's copy, p. 127.

16 It must be noted, however, that the third series, containing 166 poems, was larger than the first series (116 poems), though about the same size as the second (167 poems). Since the 1896 printer's copy survives, one can be fairly sure when a textual change was a printer's error, a misreading of the manuscripts, or an editorial alteration. A tabulation shows that within the poems that have editorial alterations some forty-six changes were made to effect a rhyme, eighteen to achieve agreement between subject and verb (including changes in mood), twelve to clarify difficult passages, five to smooth rhythm, five to regularize Emily Dickinson's use of prepositions, four to correct diction, and eleven for miscellaneous or unclear reasons.

17 M. L. Todd, unpublished journal, February 22, 1896. The correspondence dealing with the publication of these books is in the Amherst Collection, Boxes 20 and 21.

18 Todd to Hardy, December 31, 1895, quoted in *Ancestors' Brocades,* p. 334.

19 Millicent Todd Bingham discusses some of these printer's errors in *Ancestors' Brocades,* pp. 340–41. The variorum calls the transcripts in the 1896 printer's copy "uniformly accurate" (*Poems* [1955], I, xlvii) but about twenty-five of the textual changes that it lists as editorial alterations were in fact misreadings of the manuscripts or errors in transcription.

20 *Ancestors' Brocades,* pp. 342, 345.

21 Amherst Collection, Box 28.

22 1896 printer's copy, p. 128.

23 1896 printer's copy, p. 24.

24 Amherst Collection, Box 29–1. This transcript is actually not part of the 1896 printer's copy, but since it is a variant of one of the 1896 poems and it illustrates the same problem as the other poem in this paragraph, I include it here.

25 The manuscript (H 309) is at the Houghton Library.

26 It is of course possible that Mrs. Todd made her transcript from another manuscript now lost.

27 1896 printer's copy, p. 16.

28 There is also another transcript (Amherst Collection, Box 19, Tr 22) for "My life closed twice before its close" that served as copy when the poem was published in *Scribner's Magazine* (June 1896). This transcript (and also the *Scribner's* printing) is variant in the sixth line. It reads "this that twice befel" in-

stead of "these that twice befel." The paper used for this transcript is one Mrs. Todd frequently used in 1895 when making extra copies to send to magazines. The transcript is titled "Parting," is signed "Emily Dickinson" by Mrs. Todd, and has been folded from the mailing to the magazine. It is clearly not a first copy made from an original manuscript, for to them Mrs. Todd did not give titles, nor did she sign them "Emily Dickinson." This variant transcript was copied from the one in the printer's copy for the third series, to which while preparing it for press, Mrs. Todd had given the title "Parting" (see Fig. 13). The variant ("this") therefore was either a scribal error or deliberate emendation and should be discounted.

29 *Concordance* (1964), p. 77.
30 Amherst Collection, Box 19, Tr 22; see above, n. 28. This spelling was regularized in *Complete Poems* (1960), but has been continued in the *Concordance* (1964).
31 See T. W. Higginson to M. L. Todd, July 14, 1890, quoted in *Ancestors' Brocades,* p. 56; also, see discussion of this poem in Ch. IV, pp. 140–41.
32 "Disclose" has been included as Emily Dickinson's alternate in the *Concordance* (1964).
33 1896 printer's copy, pp. 167–68.
34 Millicent Todd Bingham, "Introduction," in *Bolts of Melody: New Poems of Emily Dickinson,* ed. Mabel Loomis Todd and Millicent Todd Bingham (New York: Harper, 1945), p. xi. Allowance must be made of course for copying errors, and spelling was often regularized in copying (see Ch. I).
35 1896 printer's copy, pp. 35–39.
36 Millicent Todd Bingham, "Poems of Emily Dickinson: Hitherto Published Only in Part," *New England Quarterly,* XX (March 1947), 18–19.
37 1896 printer's copy, p. 83₁.
38 Amherst Collection, Box 29–1. I am indebted to Millicent Todd Bingham for identifying her grandfather's handwriting.
39 1896 printer's copy, p. 153.
40 "Endow the Living—with the Tears" (V521) in Amherst Collection, Box 19, Tr 9; "On a Columnar Self" (V789) in Box 29–1; "A bold, inspiriting Bird" (V1177), and "The Hills in Purple syllables" (V1016) and "To die—without the Dying" (V1017) in Box 29–2.
41 Since the variorum does not include this version in the Dickinson canon, the *Concordance* (1964) does not include its variant readings.

42   *Poems* (1955), III, 1065.
43   1896 printer's copy, p. 18. As a consequence, the *Concordance* (1964) also omits "livery."
44   *Poems* (1955), III, 1183.
45   1896 printer's copy, p. 136.
46   As a consequence, the *Concordance* (1964) includes the alteration "mighty" but omits Emily Dickinson's reading "timid."
47   Since the variorum does not record the reading "fallow," the *Concordance* (1964) omits it.
48   1896 printer's copy, p. 126. Also, the comma that concludes line 11 in the variorum text of this poem should probably be a period.
49   1896 printer's copy, p. 95.
50   1896 printer's copy, p. 125.
51   As a consequence, the *Concordance* (1964) includes it as "bequeaths." *Complete Poems* (1960) repeats the error.
52   The error has been carried over into *Complete Poems* (1960) and the *Concordance* (1964).
53   1896 printer's copy, pp. 6, 101, 27, and 95.
54   1896 printer's copy, pp. 6, 101, and 27.
55   1896 printer's copy, p. 95.
56   At least one critic has tripped over this inconsistency; see Charles R. Anderson, *Emily Dickinson's Poetry: Stairway of Surprise* (New York: Holt, Rinehart and Winston, 1960), p. 122.
57   *Poems* (1955), II, 450. The manuscript (H 148c) is at the Houghton Library. Mr. Johnson gives the alternate for the eleventh line of this poem as
         we suppose] I supposed
But the pronouns are actually independent of the verb since Emily Dickinson marked "we" in the main text with a cross and entered "I" below as its alternate while she added the letter *d* directly to the word "suppose."
58   Amherst Collection, Box 1, packet 82, leaf 1.
59   Both errors discussed in this paragraph have been carried over into *Complete Poems* (1960) and the *Concordance* (1964).
60   Amherst Collection, Box 3, no. 163.
61   As a consequence of the variorum rendering, the *Concordance* (1964) does not handle "till I called" as an alternate.
       Note that there may be a similar example in the next line (14) where "and" is below "But." Though "and" appears without a majuscule, it may have been an alternate for "But."

Line 15 obliquely states the reason March is asked to forgive (the poet has not colored the hills) and should probably follow line 14 without interruption by the word "and."

62   Amherst Collection, Box 9, no. 513.

63   This much is clear. It is not clear, however, whether or not Emily Dickinson intended the substitute line to begin with the word "And." But since "we" begins with a small letter, we may conjecture that she did.

Because of the variorum rendering of this poem, the *Concordance* (1964) does not handle the alternates properly.

64   *Poems* (1955), III, 996.

65   Fair copy IV is now at the Wellesley College Library. The variorum indicates that fair copy IV was given by Mrs. Todd to Colonel Higginson, who gave it to George Herbert Palmer, and that he in turn presented it to the Wellesley College Library. Mrs. Todd, however, did not send the poem to Higginson, but sent it directly to Palmer himself. The letter of presentation (addressed to Mrs. Palmer) survives along with the manuscript in the Wellesley College Library. In the letter (February 21, 1897) Mrs. Todd said that "the enclosed poem by Emily Dickinson was sent to me many years ago, and is a characteristic bit of her later handwriting." Mr. Johnson's notes to the poem do not record that it was one that Emily Dickinson sent to Mrs. Todd, and Appendix 2 ("Tabulation of Recipients") similarly omits the fact.

66   Jay Leyda, Review of *Poems* (1955), *New England Quarterly*, XXIX (June 1956), 242.

67   It should be noted that Mr. Johnson did mark the last two poems with a star and gave them cross references to each other, though with the first two poems he did not.

68   Leyda, *New England Quarterly*, XXIX, 244.

69   The variorum has a dash concluding this line; the manuscript itself clearly has none.

70   Amherst Collection, Box 9, no. 509. This fragment also contains lines from V1425. Mr. Johnson correctly notes these lines in his discussion of V1425. He there also mentions the lines from V1213, but does not record the information in the notes to V1213 itself.

71   Amherst Collection, Box 16, no. 786. Mr. Leyda has cataloged this manuscript as one possibly sent by Emily Dickinson to Mrs. Todd.

72   Amherst Collection, Box 4, no. 226. A few manuscripts have become available since the variorum was published; a few are

for third series poems. One, the missing holograph for "Where every bird is bold to go" (V1758), has come to light in the Vassar College Library; it should now be dated and properly placed in the chronology of the poems. Also, Millicent Todd Bingham published two fragments of third series poems (V1622 and V1718) in "Prose Fragments of Emily Dickinson," *New England Quarterly,* XXVIII (September 1955), 318; they were reprinted in Mr. Johnson's edition of the *Letters* (1958), III, 921, 923.

73 The lawsuit is recounted in greater detail in *Ancestors' Brocades,* pp. 349-67. Legal records are available at the courthouse in Northampton, Massachusetts: Superior Court of Hampshire County, Massachusetts, 1898, docket nos. 125 and 193.

CHAPTER IV

1   This description is based on the arrangement of the manuscripts as of midsummer 1891 (see Ch. II).

2   *Poems* (1955), I, xlvii–xlviii.

3   *Ibid.,* I, xlviii.

4   R. P. Blackmur, "Emily Dickinson: Notes on Prejudice and Fact" [1937], in *Language as Gesture* (New York: Harcourt, Brace, 1952), p. 25.

5   The text of *Bolts of Melody,* while good, does contain errors that derive from Mrs. Todd's transcripts, which Mrs. Bingham at times had to use in lieu of the manuscripts themselves.

6   Charles R. Anderson, *Emily Dickinson's Poetry: Stairway of Surprise* (New York: Holt, Rinehart and Winston, 1960), p. 307.

7   T. W. Higginson, "Emily Dickinson's Letters," *Atlantic Monthly,* LXVIII (October 1891), 444.

8   M. L. Todd, "Preface," in *Poems* (1891), p. 6.

9   John Crowe Ransom, "Emily Dickinson: A Poet Restored," *Perspectives USA,* XV (Spring 1956), 7.

10 Anderson, *Emily Dickinson's Poetry,* p. 306. In his discussion Mr. Anderson cites articles by Mr. Blackmur and Mr. Warren: R. P. Blackmur, "Emily Dickinson's Notation," *Kenyon Review,* XVIII (Spring 1956), 224-37; Austin Warren, "Emily Dickinson," *Sewanee Review,* LXV (Autumn 1957), 565-86.

11 Edith Perry Stamm, "Emily Dickinson: Poetry and Punctuation," *Saturday Review,* XLVI (March 30, 1963), 26-27, 74.

12 *Ibid.,* p. 74.

13 *Ibid.*

14 Theodora Ward, "Poetry and Punctuation," *Saturday Review,* XLVI (April 27, 1963), 25.

15 Edith Perry Stamm, "The Punctuation Problem," *Saturday Review,* XLVI (May 25, 1963), 23.

16 Amherst Collection, Box 3, no. 175a, Box 17, no. 891 and 890, and Box 15, no. 784 respectively.

17 Amherst Collection, Box 4, no. 233a and Box 6, no. 344a.

18 Amherst Collection, Box 2, no. 126.

19 Amherst Collection, Box 8, no. 445b; Box 9, no. 510a; and Box 17, no. 889.

20 Amherst Collection, Box 8, no. 445b.

21 For example, Amherst Collection, Box 4, no. 261a, and Box 6, no. 363a.

22 Amherst Collection, Box 21.

23 Amherst Collection, Box 20, To 278–280 and To 283–284b.

24 *Poems* (1955), I, lxiii.

25 Emily Dickinson's copy of two stanzas from George Herbert's "Matins" is reproduced by Millicent Todd Bingham in *Emily Dickinson: A Revelation* (New York: Harper, 1954), p. 108.

26 Austin Warren, *Sewanee Review,* LXV, 567.

27 Kurt Oppens, "Emily Dickinson: Überlieferung und Prophetie," *Merkur,* XIV (January 1960), 27. The variorum prints V297 as follows:

> It's like the Light—
> A fashionless Delight—
> It's like the Bee—
> A dateless—Melody—
>
> It's like the Woods—
> Private—Like the Breeze—
> Phraseless—yet it stirs
> The proudest Trees—
>
> It's like the Morning—
> Best—when it's done—
> And the Everlasting Clocks—
> Chime—Noon!

28 *Ibid.*

29 Anderson, *Emily Dickinson's Poetry,* p. 304.

30 *Selected Poems of Emily Dickinson,* ed. James Reeves (London: Heinemann, 1959).

31   The third and fourth lines in Reeves' text read:

> You may have met him—did you not?
> His notice sudden is.

The third line had been exactly the same when it was first published in the *Springfield Daily Republican* (February 14, 1866),
and Emily Dickinson wrote to Colonel Higginson that "it was
robbed of me—defeated too of the third line by the punctuation. The third and fourth were one . . . ." (*Letters* [1958],
II, 450.) There should be no question mark at the end of the
third line in this poem; if anything, a comma.

The variorum notes to this poem are erroneous where they
cite the *SDR* version. Line 3 in *SDR* ends with a question mark,
line 4 ends with a comma, and line 21 varies textually from
the packet copy—contrary to what the variorum notes say. See
also John L. Spicer, "The Poems of Emily Dickinson," *Boston
Public Library Quarterly*, VIII (July 1956), 142–43. According
to Mr. Spicer, Emily Dickinson included a clipping of this
poem from the *Springfield Weekly Republican* (February 17,
1866), not from the *Daily Republican,* when she wrote to
Higginson complaining about the punctuation. Apparently
relying on the variorum notes, Mr. Spicer indicates that the
Weekly differed from the *Daily* in the punctuation of lines 3–4
as well as in the text of line 21. Both printings, however, are
available in the Amherst College Library holdings of this newspaper, and they are identical. The verso of the clipping Emily
Dickinson sent to Higginson discloses that it was in fact taken
from the *Daily.* Cf. also the account in *Letters* (1958), II, 451.

32   Newton Arvin, Review of *Poems* (1955), *American Literature,*
XXVIII (May 1956), 234.

33   See W. W. Greg, "The Rationale of Copy-Text," *Studies in
Bibliography,* III (1950–51), 19–36, and Fredson Bowers,
"Current Theories of Copy-Text, With an Illustration from
Dryden," *Modern Philology,* XLVIII (August 1950), 12–20.

34   William M. Gibson and Edwin H. Cady, "Editions of American Writers, 1963: A Preliminary Survey," *PMLA,* LXXVIII,
no. 4, pt. 2 (September 1963), 8.

35   *Letters* (1958), II, 408.

36   Thomas H. Johnson, *Emily Dickinson: An Interpretive Biography* (Cambridge: Harvard University Press, 1955), pp. 103–
14.

37   *Poems* (1955), I, lxi.

38   At times Mr. Johnson followed another principle: "If a poem seems to achieve its final version at a date later than that of earlier fair copies, it is placed among poems written during the later year" (*Poems* [1955], I, lxi–lxii). This "final version" is apparently not the same as a version established by the final intention of the author, but rather a higher evolution of the poem as poem.

39   *Poems* (1955), I, xxxiii.

40   This is a general description. The form of some semifinal drafts differs, and not all are in the packets.

41   *Poems* (1955), I, xxxv.

42   Thomas H. Johnson, "Establishing a Text: The Emily Dickinson Papers," *Studies in Bibliography*, V (1952–53), 31–32. The italics are Mr. Johnson's.

43   *Poems* (1955), I, xxxv, and III, 839–40.

44   *Ibid.*, I, xxxv.

45   See, for example, the reviews of the variorum by Newton Arvin, R. P. Blackmur, John Crowe Ransom, Louis Untermeyer, and Austin Warren.

46   *Poems* (1955), III, 995–98. For a discussion of the correct text of fair copy IV, see Ch. III, pp. 107–9.

47   *Ibid.*, I, xxxv.

48   There is an inconsistency here in Mr. Johnson's position. In the paper read before the English Institute he concluded that even fair copies have no final intention if the poet allowed the packet versions to stand with alternate readings. The packet version of "A Dew sufficed itself" is a semifinal draft.

49   Cf. Mr. Johnson's statement in *Poems* (1955), I, xxxiv: "Indeed, the fair copies themselves seem to have been considered alterable as long as they remained packet copies."

50   On the subject of establishing "the canon of her highest achievement," see Anderson, *Emily Dickinson's Poetry*, pp. x–xii.

51   For examples, see *ibid.*

52   *Complete Poems* (1960), p. x. It should be noted, however, that only one version of V228 appears in the text.

53   *Ibid.*

54   *Poems* (1955), I, xxxiii.

55   *Ibid.*, I, xxxv.

56   *Ibid.*

57   Any editor of Emily Dickinson after 1955 necessarily faced the same problems that Mr. Johnson did when he prepared his 1960 volume. I have examined over a dozen selected editions pub-

lished since then, and none of them has faced up to the textual difficulties. Several follow Mr. Johnson's arbitrary policy of reprinting the principal representation of the variorum. Others revert to the work of the nineteenth-century editors, now in public domain, and in doing so reproduce texts containing a good many editorial alterations.

While it is not really an edition, Charles R. Anderson suggests his critical work, *Emily Dickinson's Poetry: Stairway of Surprise* (1960), be considered as a little anthology, since he prints one full text of each poem that he criticizes. Recognizing that there is no authorial final intention, he has chosen freely from the alternates in constructing his readings of the poems.

58   John Ciardi, "Out of the Top Drawer," *Nation,* CLXXXI (November 5, 1955), 398.

59   Robert Hillyer, "What Emily Really Wrote," *New York Times Book Review,* LX (September 11, 1955), 7.

60   *Poems* (1955), I, xxxv.

61   Ronald B. McKerrow, ed., *The Works of Thomas Nashe,* 5 vols. (London: A. H. Bullen; and Sidgwick and Jackson, 1904–10), II, 196. For reappraisal of McKerrow's general editorial position, see W. W. Greg, "McKerrow's Prolegomena Reconsidered," *Review of English Studies,* XVII (April 1941), 139–49, and Fredson Bowers, "McKerrow's Editorial Principles for Shakespeare Reconsidered," *Shakespeare Quarterly,* VI (Summer 1955), 309–24.

62   Chauncey Sanders, *An Introduction to Research in English Literary History* (New York: Macmillan, 1952), pp. 112–13. See also André Morize, *Problems and Methods of Literary History* (Boston: Ginn, 1922), pp. 53–54. At present editors generally would choose the edition closest to the manuscript source, but they would incorporate into it later readings that can be shown to have authority.

63   Malcolm Cowley, ed., *Leaves of Grass: The First (1855) Edition,* by Walt Whitman (New York: Viking Press, 1959), p. x.

64   Gibson and Cady, *PMLA,* LXXVIII, 1.

65   They are in (1) *Poems* (1891), ed. T. W. Higginson and Mabel Loomis Todd, (2) *Selected Poems* (1959), ed. James Reeves, and *Poesie* (1959), ed. Guido Errante, (3) *Complete Poems* (1960), ed. Thomas H. Johnson, (4) Anderson, *Emily Dickinson's Poetry,* p. 15.

66   Anderson, *Emily Dickinson's Poetry,* p. 15.

67   See *Ancestors' Brocades,* p. 56. The stanza is quoted from *Poems* (1890), p. 100.

68   Allen Tate, "Emily Dickinson" [1932], in *Collected Essays* (Denver: Swallow, 1959), pp. 205–6.

69   See *Poems* (1955), II, 546–47.

70   George F. Whicher, *This Was a Poet: A Critical Biography of Emily Dickinson* (New York: Scribner's, 1938), pp. 202–3.

71   See *Poems* (1955), I, 53–54.

72   The twenty-six possibilities fit the eleven positions in the poem in this way: (1) 2, (2) 2, (3) 5, (4) 2, (5) 2, (6) 2, (7) 2, (8) 2, (9) 2, (10) 2, (11) 3. Since the substitutions are independent of each other, the number of possible combinations is the product of the factors, and 2 x 2 x 5 x 2 x 2 x 2 x 2 x 2 x 2 x 2 x 3 = 7680.

Bibliography

I. PRIMARY SOURCES

The main collections used in preparing this book are at the Amherst College Library and the Houghton Library of Harvard University. Most of Emily Dickinson's poems and letters are at these libraries. The Amherst College Library also has Mabel Loomis Todd's transcripts of the poems, her editorial correspondence with Thomas Wentworth Higginson, the 1891 notebook, and other material relevant to the early editing. Colonel Higginson deposited his papers in the Boston Public Library, and several Emily Dickinson holographs are among them. A few relevant holographs are located in the Vassar College Library, the Wellesley College Library, and the Library of Congress.

The World typewriter, on which Mabel Loomis Todd made many of the transcripts, is now at the Jones Library, Amherst, Massachusetts. Records pertaining to the Dickinson-Todd lawsuit are available at the courthouse in Northampton (Superior Court of Hampshire County, Massachusetts, 1898, docket nos. 125 and 193). The diaries and journals of Mabel Loomis Todd, as well as other family papers in the possession of Millicent Todd Bingham, are in the process of transfer to the Yale University Library.

II. MAIN EDITIONS

Poems by Emily Dickinson, ed. Mabel Loomis Todd and T. W. Higginson. Boston: Roberts Brothers, 1890.
Poems by Emily Dickinson, ed. T. W. Higginson and Mabel Loomis Todd. Second Series. Boston: Roberts Brothers, 1891.

Letters of Emily Dickinson, ed. Mabel Loomis Todd. 2 vols. Boston: Roberts Brothers, 1894.

Poems by Emily Dickinson, ed. Mabel Loomis Todd. Third Series. Boston: Roberts Brothers, 1896.

The Single Hound, ed. Martha Dickinson Bianchi. Boston: Little, Brown, 1914.

The Complete Poems of Emily Dickinson, ed. Martha Dickinson Bianchi and Alfred Leete Hampson. Boston: Little, Brown, 1924.

Further Poems of Emily Dickinson, ed. Martha Dickinson Bianchi and Alfred Leete Hampson. Boston: Little, Brown, 1929.

The Poems of Emily Dickinson, ed. Martha Dickinson Bianchi and Alfred Leete Hampson. Boston: Little, Brown, 1930.

Letters of Emily Dickinson, ed. Mabel Loomis Todd. New and enlarged edition. New York: Harper, 1931.

Unpublished Poems of Emily Dickinson, ed. Martha Dickinson Bianchi and Alfred Leete Hampson. Boston: Little, Brown, 1935.

Poems by Emily Dickinson, ed. Martha Dickinson Bianchi and Alfred Leete Hampson. Boston: Little, Brown, 1937.

Bolts of Melody: New Poems of Emily Dickinson, ed. Mabel Loomis Todd and Millicent Todd Bingham. New York: Harper, 1945.

Emily Dickinson's Letters to Dr. and Mrs. Josiah Gilbert Holland, ed. Theodora Van Wagenen Ward. Cambridge: Harvard University Press, 1951.

The Poems of Emily Dickinson, ed. Thomas H. Johnson. 3 vols. Cambridge: Harvard University Press, 1955.

The Letters of Emily Dickinson, ed. Thomas H. Johnson and Theodora Ward. 3 vols. Cambridge: Harvard University Press, 1958.

The Complete Poems of Emily Dickinson, ed. Thomas H. Johnson. Boston: Little, Brown, 1960.

Final Harvest: Emily Dickinson's Poems, ed. Thomas H. Johnson. Boston: Little, Brown, 1962.

III. OTHER WORKS CITED

Aldrich, Thomas Bailey. *"In Re* Emily Dickinson," *Atlantic Monthly,* LXIX (January 1892), 143–44.

Anderson, Charles R. *Emily Dickinson's Poetry: Stairway of Surprise.* New York: Holt, Rinehart and Winston, 1960.

Arvin, Newton. Review of *The Poems of Emily Dickinson,* ed. Thomas H. Johnson, *American Literature,* XXVIII (May 1956), 232–36.

Bates, Arlo. "Miss Dickinson's Poems," *Boston Courier,* November 23, 1890.

Bingham, Millicent Todd. *Ancestors' Brocades: The Literary Debut of Emily Dickinson*. New York: Harper, 1945.
————. *Emily Dickinson: A Revelation*. New York: Harper, 1954.
————. *Emily Dickinson's Home: Letters of Edward Dickinson and His Family*. New York: Harper, 1955.
————. *Mabel Loomis Todd: Her Contributions to the Town of Amherst*. New York: privately printed, 1935.
————. "Poems of Emily Dickinson: Hitherto Published Only in Part," *New England Quarterly*, XX (March 1947), 3–50.
————. "Prose Fragments of Emily Dickinson," *New England Quarterly*, XXVIII (September 1955), 291–318.
Blackmur, R. P. "Emily Dickinson's Notation," *Kenyon Review*, XVIII (Spring 1956), 224–37.
————. *Language as Gesture*. New York: Harcourt, Brace, 1952.
Bowers, Fredson. "Current Theories of Copy-Text, With an Illustration from Dryden," *Modern Philology*, XLVIII (August 1950), 12–20.
————. "McKerrow's Editorial Principles for Shakespeare Reconsidered," *Shakespeare Quarterly*, VI (Summer 1955), 309–24.
Chamberlain, Arthur. "The Poems of Emily Dickinson," *The Commonwealth* (Boston), December 26, 1891.
Ciardi, John. "Out of the Top Drawer," *Nation*, CLXXXI (November 5, 1955), 397–98.
Dickinson, Emily. *Poesie*, ed. Guido Errante. 2 vols. Verona: Mondadori, 1959.
————. *Selected Poems of Emily Dickinson*, ed. James Reeves. London: Heinemann, 1959.
"Emily Dickinson's Poems," *People and Patriot* (Concord, N.H.), February 1892.
Gibson, William M., and Edwin H. Cady. "Editions of American Writers, 1963: A Preliminary Survey," *PMLA*, LXXVIII, no. 4, pt. 2 (September 1963), 1–8.
Greg, W. W. "McKerrow's Prolegomena Reconsidered," *Review of English Studies*, XVII (April 1941), 139–49.
————. "The Rationale of Copy-Text," *Studies in Bibliography*, III (1950–51), 19–36.
Higgins, David J. M. "Twenty-five Poems by Emily Dickinson: Unpublished Variant Versions," *American Literature*, XXXVIII (March 1966), 1–21.
Higginson, Thomas Wentworth. "Emily Dickinson's Letters," *Atlantic Monthly*, LXVIII (October 1891), 444–56.
————. "An Open Portfolio," *Christian Union*, XLII (September 25, 1890), 392–93.

Hillyer, Robert. "What Emily Really Wrote," *New York Times Book Review*, LX (September 11, 1955), 7.

Howells, William Dean. "Editor's Study," *Harper's Magazine*, LXXXII (January 1891), 316–21.

Johnson, Thomas H. "Establishing a Text: The Emily Dickinson Papers," *Studies in Bibliography*, V (1952–53), 21–32.

———. *Emily Dickinson: An Interpretive Biography*. Cambridge: Harvard University Press, 1955.

Leyda, Jay. Review of *The Poems of Emily Dickinson*, ed. Thomas H. Johnson, *New England Quarterly*, XXIX (June 1956), 239–45.

———. *The Years and Hours of Emily Dickinson*. 2 vols. New Haven: Yale University Press, 1960.

Morize, André. *Problems and Methods of Literary History*. Boston: Ginn, 1922.

Moulton, Louise Chandler. "A Very Remarkable Book," *Boston Sunday Herald*, November 23, 1890.

Nashe, Thomas. *The Works of Thomas Nashe*, ed. Ronald B. McKerrow. 5 vols. London: A. H. Bullen; and Sidgwick and Jackson, 1904–10.

"The Newest Poet," *Daily News* (London), January 2, 1891.

Oppens, Kurt. "Emily Dickinson: Überlieferung und Prophetie," *Merkur*, XIV (January 1960), 17–40.

Ransom, John Crowe. "Emily Dickinson: A Poet Restored," *Perspectives USA*, XV (Spring 1956), 5–20.

Rosenbaum, S. P., ed. *A Concordance to the Poems of Emily Dickinson*. Ithaca: Cornell University Press, 1964.

Sanders, Chauncey. *An Introduction to Research in English Literary History*. New York: Macmillan, 1952.

Spicer, John L. "The Poems of Emily Dickinson," *Boston Public Library Quarterly*, VIII (July 1956), 135–43.

Stamm, Edith Perry. "Emily Dickinson: Poetry and Punctuation," *Saturday Review*, XLVI (March 30, 1963), 26–27, 74.

———. "The Punctuation Problem," *Saturday Review*, XLVI (May 25, 1963), 23.

Tate, Allen. *Collected Essays*. Denver: Swallow, 1959.

Todd, Mabel Loomis. "Emily Dickinson's Letters," *Bachelor of Arts*, I (May 1895), 39–66.

———. "Emily Dickinson's Literary Début," *Harper's Magazine*, CLX (March 1930), 463–71.

Untermeyer, Louis. "The Compleat Spinster Poet," *Saturday Review*, XXXVIII (September 10, 1955), 37–39.

Ward, Theodora. "Poetry and Punctuation," *Saturday Review*, XLVI (April 27, 1963), 25.

Warren, Austin. "Emily Dickinson," *Sewanee Review*, LXV (Autumn 1957), 565–86.

Wells, Anna Mary. *Dear Preceptor: The Life and Times of Thomas Wentworth Higginson.* Boston: Houghton Mifflin, 1963.

Whicher, George Frisbie. *This Was a Poet: A Critical Biography of Emily Dickinson.* New York: Scribner's, 1938.

Whiting, Lilian. "Poems," *Boston Budget*, November 23, 1890.

Whitman, Walt. *Leaves of Grass: The First (1855) Edition*, ed. Malcolm Cowley. New York: Viking Press, 1959.

Index

Aldrich, Thomas Bailey: on ED, 27

Alterations, editorial. *See* Higginson, Thomas Wentworth; Todd, Mabel Loomis

Amherst, Massachusetts, 4, 5, 6, 7, 20, 26, 81, 114 116, 121, 148*n*15, 149*n*27, 158*n*63

Amherst Academy, 119

Amherst College, 4, 34. *See also* Manuscripts, ED's

Anderson, Charles R.: on ED's punctuation and capitalization, 117, 118, 121, 126; ED texts, 139–40, 168–69*n*57; on "I like to hear it lap the Miles," 140; mentioned, 163*n*56

Aristotelian approach to criticism, 141–42

Arvin, Newton: on ED's punctuation, 128; mentioned, 168*n*45

Atlantic Monthly, 27, 117

Bachelor of Arts: ED poems in, 160*n*8

Bates, Arlo: markings on transcripts, 17; numbering of poems, 17, 21, 150*n*41, 151*n*43; on ED's poetry, 20–21; on editing ED, 21, 23, 24; and selection for *Poems* (1890), 21–22, 150*n*41, 151*n*43; review of *Poems* (1890), 26; mentioned, 28

"Because I could not stop for Death"

(V712): Tate on, 141; editorial alteration of, 141

Bianchi, Martha Dickinson: and mutilation of manuscripts, 34; and H 157, 44–45; ED editions by, 44, 95–97, 112, 115–16, 160*n*8; and "S.H.D.'s copy—", 88; death of, 116; heir of, 116

Bingham, Millicent Todd: notes on transcripts, 17; on Bates, 21; and mutilation of manuscripts, 34; manuscript gifts by, 34, 48, 116; numbering of envelopes, 35, 36 156*n*46; text of "I tie my Hat—I crease my Shawl," 42; on M. L. Todd's copying habits, 91; text of "I measure every Grief I meet," 91; ED editions by, 116, 165*n*5; term for "packet," 147*n*4; on numbering of packets, 149*n*23; mentioned, 161*n*19, 162*n*38, 164*n*72, 166*n*25

Blackmur, R. P.: on ED editions, 116; mentioned, 118, 165*n*10, 168*n*45

"Blazing in Gold and quenching in Purple" (V228): in *Complete Poems* (1960), 133, 168*n*52

"Bless God, he went as soldiers" (V147): belongs to packet 80, 68–72; holograph of, 69; transcript of, 72, 157*n*53; dating of, 74

177